# *Contents*

Preface iv

Acknowledgements vi

**Chapter 1** Introducing chemistry 1
**Chapter 2** The world of matter 15
**Chapter 3** Separation of mixtures 33
**Chapter 4** Elements and atoms 47
**Chapter 5** Chemical reactions 57
**Chapter 6** Acids and bases 69
**Chapter 7** Air 77
**Chapter 8** The Earth – a rocky planet 91
**Chapter 9** Metals and non-metals 104
**Chapter 10** Earth materials 120
**Chapter 11** The chemical industry 139
**Chapter 12** Chemicals and the environment 150
**Chapter 13** The periodic table 167
**Chapter 14** Using formulae 176

Glossary 179

Index 182

# *Preface*

## To the pupil

Chemistry is the scientific study of matter and materials. These are substances such as air, water and rock, which make our world. Matter is made from tiny structures called atoms that join together in many different ways to make millions of different kinds of chemicals.

The first atoms formed at the beginning of the Universe. At that time a huge explosion called the Big Bang took place. The first atoms formed two gases – hydrogen and helium. Over thousands of millions of years since then many other atoms were made in the stars. When the stars faded out or exploded in a super nova these atoms spread through space and formed dust. In time, one cloud of dust formed the Solar System and everything that is in it. This means that all the materials you will study in your chemistry course once formed in the Universe billions of years ago. It also means that the materials from which you are made formed then too.

Our knowledge of chemistry has developed from the observations, investigations and ideas of many people over a long period of time. Today this knowledge is increasing rapidly as there are more chemists – people who study matter and materials – than ever before.

In the past, few people other then scientists were informed about the latest discoveries. Today, through newspapers and television, everyone can learn about the latest discoveries on a wide range of chemical topics, from making new materials for exploring the oceans or space, and developing new medicines and fuels, to finding ways to recycle the materials we use to make them available for future generations.

*Chemistry Now! 11–14* covers the requirements of your examinations in a way that I hope will help you understand how observations, investigations and ideas have led to the scientific facts we use today. The questions are set to help you extract information from what you read and see, and to help you think more deeply about each chapter in this book. Some questions are set so you can discuss your ideas with others and develop a point of view on different scientific issues. This should help you in the future when new scientific issues, which are as yet unknown, affect your life.

# Chemistry
# NOW!
## 11–14

## Peter D Riley

**JOHN MURRAY**

Titles in this series:

*Chemistry Now! 11–14* Pupil's Book ISBN 0 7195 7546 X
*Chemistry Now! 11–14* Teacher's Resource Book ISBN 0 7195 7547 8
*Biology Now! 11–14* Pupil's Book ISBN 0 7195 7548 6
*Biology Now! 11–14* Teacher's Resource Book ISBN 0 7195 7549 4
*Physics Now! 11–14* Pupil's Book ISBN 0 7195 7544 3
*Physics Now! 11–14* Teacher's Resource Book ISBN 0 7195 7545 1

First published in 1999
by John Murray (Publishers) Ltd
50 Albemarle Street
London W1X 4BD

Layouts by Black Dog Design
Artwork by Barking Dog Art, Linden Artists and
Richard Duszczak
Cover design by John Townson/Creation

Typeset in 12/14 pt Garamond Light by Wearset,
Boldon, Tyne and Wear.
Printed and bound by G. Canale, Italy

A catalogue entry for this title is available from the
British Library

ISBN 0 7195 7546 X

The scientific activities of thinking up ideas to test and carrying out investigations are enjoyed so much by many people that they take up a career in science. Perhaps *Chemistry Now! 11–14* may help you to take up a career in science too.

## To the teacher

*Chemistry Now! 11–14* has been written to cover the requirements of the curriculum for the Common Entrance Examination at 13+, the National Curriculum for Science at Key Stage 3 and equivalent junior courses. It aims to help pupils to become more scientifically literate by encouraging them to examine the information in the text and illustrations in order to answer questions about them in a variety of ways. The book presents science as a human activity by considering the development of scientific ideas from the earliest times to present day, and deals with applications of scientific knowledge and issues that arise from them.

*Chemistry Now! 11–14* and its supporting *Teacher's Resource Book* are designed to provide the chemistry content of a balanced science course in which biology, chemistry and physics are taught separately. It may also be used as a supplementary text in more integrated courses to demonstrate aspects of science as a human activity and to extend skills in comprehension.

# *Acknowledgements*

I would like to thank Katie Mackenzie Stuart and Julie Jones for their encouragement, help and support throughout the preparation of this book.

The following are sources from which artwork and tables have been adapted or redrawn:

Figure 3.5 **p.36** from *Letts Key Stage 3 Study Guide: Science* by B. McDuell & G. Booth, by permission of Letts Educational.
Figure A **p.47** from Figure 5 of *Alchemy* by E.J. Holmyard, Penguin (1957).
Table 9.2 **p.111** from Figure 6.2 of *Chemistry Today* by Euan Henderson, Macmillan.

The following have supplied photographs or have given permission for photographs to be reproduced:

**Cover** Tek Image/Science Photo Library; **p.1** *left* Science Museum/Science & Society Picture Library, *right* Geoff Tompkinson/Science Photo Library; **p.2** Andrew Lambert; **p.3** *both* Andrew Lambert; **p.4** Andrew Lambert; **p.5** *top* Andrew Lambert, *bottom* Damien Lovegrove/Science Photo Library; **p.6** *all* Andrew Lambert; **p.7** Science Museum/Science & Society Picture Library; **p.8** Andrew Lambert; **p.13** *top* David Taylor/Science Photo Library, *bottom* Louise Lockley/CSIRO/Science Photo Library; **p.14** Ecoscene/Sally Morgan; **p.16** Peter Menzel/Science Photo Library; **p.17** *top* John Townson/Creation, *bottom* The Stock Market Photo Agency Inc.; **p.18** John Townson/Creation; **p.21** John Townson/Creation; **p.22** Albert/Rex Features; **p.25** Heather Angel; **p.26** *top* John Townson/Creation, *bottom* Andrew Lambert; **p.29** John Townson/Creation; **p.30** Mary Evans Picture Library; **p.31** *all* Andrew Lambert; **p.34** *top* David Woodfall/NHPA, *bottom* Biophoto Associates/Science Photo Library; **p.35** *all* Andrew Lambert; **p.39** John Townson/Creation; **p.41** *both* Andrew Lambert; **p.45** *both* John Townson/Creation; **p.51** *top* Andrew Lambert, *bottom* Mary Evans Picture Library; **p.54** Alfred Pasieka/Science Photo Library; **p.55** Wellcome Institute Library, London; **p.58** John Townson/Creation; **p.59** *top* John Townson/ Creation, *bottom* Mary Evans Picture Library; **p.60** *all* Andrew Lambert; **p.61** *all* Andrew Lambert; **p.63** John Townson/Creation; **p.64** Juhan Kuus/Rex Features; **p.66** *top* Andrew Lambert, *bottom* John Townson/Creation; **p.69** *left* John Townson/ Creation, *centre* Planet Earth Pictures/Philip Chapman, *right* John Townson/Creation; **p.70** Andrew Lambert; **p.72** *top* John Townson/Creation, *bottom left* Planet Earth Pictures/Pete Atkinson, *bottom right* Planet Earth Pictures/Ken Lucas; **p.73** Andrew Lambert; **p.75** *top* John Townson/Creation, *bottom* Ecoscene/Gryniewicz; **p.76** Andrew Lambert; **p.78** Greg Bartley/BOC Group; **p.79** Tek Image/Science Photo Library; **p.80** Planet Earth Pictures/Flip Schulke; **p.81** *top* Mark Brewer/Rex Features, *bottom* David Parker/Science Photo Library; **p.82** *top* Mark Beltran/People in Pictures, *bottom left* John Townson/Creation, *bottom right* Peter Knab/ Sainsbury's *The Magazine*; **p.88** Science Museum/Science & Society Picture Library; **p.89** John Townson/Creation; **p.91** John Townson/Creation; **p.94** *top* Planet Earth Pictures/ I & V Krafft, *bottom* Geoscience Features Picture Library; **p.95** *both* Geoscience Features Picture Library; **p.96** John Townson/Creation; **p.97** *all* Geoscience Features Picture Library; **p.98** *all* Geoscience Features Picture Library; **p.99** *both* Geoscience Features Picture Library; **p.100** Geoscience Features Picture Library; **p.101** Martin Bond/Science Photo Library; **p.105** *both* Geoscience Features Picture Library; **p.107** *both* Andrew Lambert; **p.109** Andrew Lambert; **p.110** *both* Andrew Lambert; **p.112** The Science Museum/Science & Society Picture Library; **p.113** Mary Evans Picture Library; **p.116** Andrew Lambert; **p.120** *all* Geoscience Features Picture Library; **p.121** Gerald Cubitt/Bruce Coleman Ltd; **p.122** John Townson/ Creation; **p.123** John Townson/Creation; **p.124** *top* BICC Cables Limited, *bottom* Ronald Sheridan/Ancient Art and Architecture Collection; **p.125** Larry Mulvehill/Science Photo Library; **p.128** Robert Harding Picture Library; **p.129** Jaguar Cars Limited; **p.131** John Townson/ Creation; **p.135** Royal Institute of British Architects; **p.137** Andrew Lambert; **p.139** *both* University of Bradford; **p.140** *top* Weston Point Studios Limited, *bottom* John Watney; **p.142** John Townson/Creation; **p.144** Simon Fraser/Science Photo Library; **p.145** Ecoscene/Adrian Morgan; **p.151** Mary Evans Picture Library; **p.152** *top* Giles Angel/Biofotos, *bottom* John Townson/Creation; **p.155** Heather Angel; **p.156** Hulton Getty; **p.157** Robert Harding Picture Library; **p.158** Astrid & Hanns-Frieder Michler/Science Photo Library; **p.159** Geoscience Features Picture Library; **p.160** Ecoscene/Alexandra Jones; **p.161** Ecoscene/Kieran Murray; **p.162** *top* Ecoscene/Sally Morgan, *bottom* Ecoscene/W. Lawler; **p.163** Ecoscene/Chinch Gryniewicz; **p.165** John Townson/Creation; **p.166** NASA/Science Photo Library; **p.167** Science Photo Library; **p.170** Science Photo Library; **p.171** *both* Geoscience Features Picture Library; **p.172** Tony Stone Worldwide; **p.173** Geoff Tompkinson/Science Photo Library; **p.174** Paul Brierley Photo Library; **p.175** *both* © ILFORD Imaging; **p.176** *both* Adam Hart-Davis/Science Photo Library; **p.177** Will and Deni McIntyre/Science Photo Library.

The publishers have made every effort to contact copyright holders. If any have been overlooked they will make the necessary arrangements at the earliest opportunity.

# 1 Introducing chemistry

## What is chemistry?

Chemistry is the study of the structure of substances and how they change. It developed out of a human activity called alchemy, which was practised in Europe, China and India for over a thousand years.

Alchemy was the study of matter, but the ideas the alchemists used in their work were not based on scientific investigations. They believed that there was a substance called the philosopher's stone which could change metals such as lead into gold. Alchemists performed experiments on a wide range of substances to try to find the philosopher's stone. They kept notes of their work, but used strange symbols to keep their work secret. The mysterious way in which they worked, and the coloured flames, explosions, smoke and fumes they made, meant they became known as magicians and wizards. None of them ever found the philosopher's stone and by the 17th Century, scientific investigations had replaced the alchemists' experiments. Some of the alchemists' knowledge was used by the first chemists who based their conclusions on what they observed and not on ideas about changing lead into gold.

**Figure 1.1**  An alchemist at work.

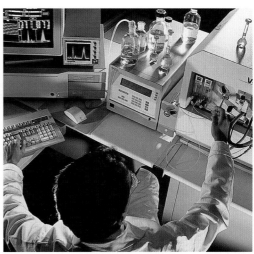

**Figure 1.2**  A present day chemist at work.

1 One of the first observations of how things change was made by people watching a fire burn. What changes occur when wood burns?

2 Why do you think that alchemists wanted to keep their work secret?

Today, chemistry and the work of chemists affects our lives in many ways; from the paper, ink and glue in this book, to the food in the last meal you ate and the fibres and colours of the clothes you are wearing now.

# Measuring quantities

For many investigations, the quantities of substances taking part in a chemical reaction need to be known and also the quantities of the substances that are produced.

## Measuring volumes of liquids

The volume of a liquid can be found by pouring it into a measuring cylinder and reading the scale. A measuring cylinder can also be used to prepare a specified volume of a liquid by pouring in an amount of the liquid, then either topping it up or pouring some out, until the required volume is present in the cylinder.

A burette is used to deliver a required volume of liquid, but it cannot be used to find the volume of a liquid in the same way that a measuring cylinder can.

The scales on measuring cylinders and burettes indicate the volume in either millilitres (ml) or cubic centimetres ($cm^3$). A millilitre is a thousandth of a litre and is used in measuring out liquids that are sold in bottles and cans. It is also used to indicate the quantities of liquids that are used in recipes. In scientific work the unit $cm^3$ is used. $1 cm^3 = 1 ml$.

### *Measuring cylinder*

A liquid is poured into the cylinder and the volume is read from the scale on the side. The surface of the liquid curves upwards at the point where it touches the inside of the cylinder. This curvature is called the meniscus. To read the volume of a liquid accurately, the base of the measuring cylinder must be placed on a flat surface and the eye must be level with the surface of the liquid in the middle of the cylinder (see Figure 1.3). The volume of liquid in the cylinder is $35 cm^3$.

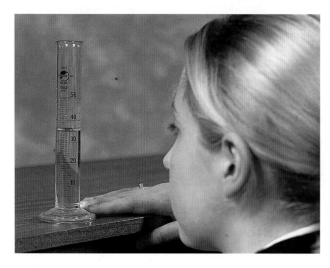

**Figure 1.3** Reading the volume of liquid in a measuring cylinder.

**3** How would reading the volume of the liquid from the top of the meniscus make the reading inaccurate?

The meniscus of mercury is unusual in that it curves downwards. You would never measure mercury in a measuring cylinder (too dangerous), but you can see its meniscus in a mercury-in-glass thermometer.

### *Burette*

The liquid is poured into the top and the burette is filled up to the zero mark on the scale. Liquid is drawn from the burette by opening the tap at the bottom (see Figure 1.4). The amount of liquid that has been released from the burette is $11\,cm^3$.

## Measuring the volume of a gas

The volume of a gas may be measured using a syringe with a scale marked on it. The scale may measure in millilitres or cubic centimetres. As the gas is produced it passes along a tube into the syringe and pushes out the plunger. The volume collected in the syringe can be measured by reading the scale at the place where the plunger comes to rest (see Figure 1.5).

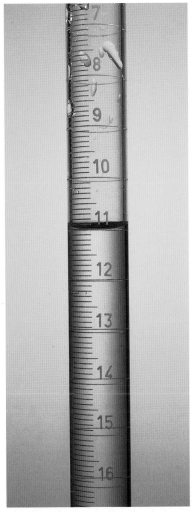

**Figure 1.4** A burette scale reads from the top down.

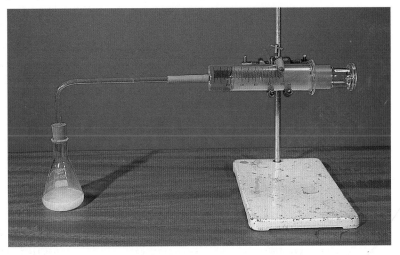

**Figure 1.5** A syringe containing a gas.

## Measuring the mass of a solid or liquid

The mass of a substance can be found by using a top loading balance. This piece of equipment is very sensitive and must be treated with great care at all times. Loads for weighing must be put onto, and removed from, the pan carefully.

The mass of the substance in Figure 1.6 is found by reading the main number display and then reading the two decimal places from the second number display. The mass of the substance in Figure 1.6 is $17.24\,g$.

**Figure 1.6**  A top loading balance.

The top loading balance measures mass in grams (g) but it also has a mechanism which allows larger masses to be measured in kilograms (kg). For most laboratory work the balance is used to measure small masses in grams.

If a substance such as a liquid is to be weighed in a beaker, the mass of the beaker must first be found. The mass of the substance and the beaker is then found, and the mass of the substance is calculated by subtracting the mass of the beaker from this total. For example:

$$\text{mass of beaker} = 50.00 \text{ g}$$
$$\text{mass of beaker} + \text{substance} = 120.00 \text{ g}$$
$$\text{mass of substance} = 120.00 - 50.00 = 70.00 \text{ g}$$

Some balances have a tare. This mechanism allows substances to be weighed out without having to make a calculation. It is used in the following way: the empty beaker is placed on the top pan and its mass is displayed. The tare is then used by turning or pushing a control on the side of the balance. This action brings the reading on the balance back to zero, even though the beaker is still on the pan. The substance can then be placed in the beaker and its mass is read directly from the display.

## Measuring temperature

The thermometer is used to measure temperature (see Figure 1.7). It is a glass tube, with a small container called a bulb at one end. In the container is a liquid which expands or contracts as the temperature changes. The liquid may be mercury or coloured alcohol.

A small amount of the liquid forms a thread in the thermometer tube. As the temperature rises the liquid expands and the thread in the tube increases in length. When the temperature falls the liquid contracts and the thread decreases in length. The length of the thread is measured on a scale on the tube. The Celsius scale is used on most laboratory thermometers. This scale is used to measure the temperature in degrees Celsius (°C).

The end of the thermometer that does not have the bulb may be capped with a piece of plastic, designed to stop the thermometer rolling along the bench and falling onto the floor. Some people fail to tell the difference between the cap and the bulb when they first use a thermometer and use it the wrong way up!

When the temperature of a liquid is to be measured, the bulb of the thermometer should be put into the liquid and the movement of the mercury or coloured alcohol in the thermometer observed. When the expansion or contraction is finished, the temperature can be read from the scale. While the temperature is being read the bulb of the thermometer must be kept immersed in the liquid. If it is removed the temperature of the air will be recorded.

When the temperature of a human is taken, a clinical thermometer may be used (see Figure 1.8). The thermometer is left in place for a few minutes before the temperature is read. It can be removed from the patient for reading because it has a narrow bend in the tube which prevents the mercury, which has expanded along the scale, from returning to the bulb. When the thermometer has been read, the mercury is moved back to the bulb by shaking the thermometer.

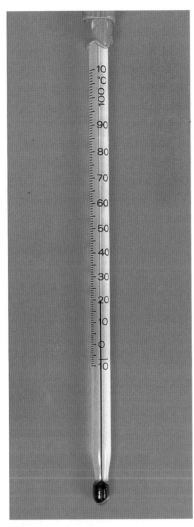

**Figure 1.7** A thermometer.

4 What temperature does the thermometer in Figure 1.7 show?

5 Someone is asked to take the temperature of a liquid. They put the bulb of the thermometer in the liquid for a few minutes, then take it out to read it. Will their reading be accurate? Explain your answer.

6 What advice would you give to someone who was taking the temperature of a liquid?

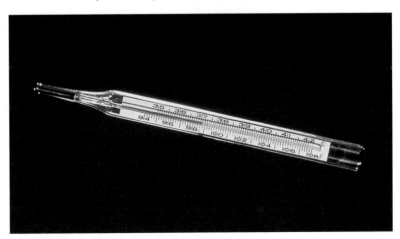

**Figure 1.8** A clinical thermometer.

# Apparatus

The equipment that is used in a chemistry laboratory is called apparatus. Many pieces of apparatus are made of glass because it is transparent, so the chemical reactions are easy to see. Glass is also easy to clean. The ordinary glass used in objects found in the home breaks if it is heated. The glass apparatus used in the laboratory is usually made from borosilicate glass, also known as Pyrex. This glass does not break when it is heated. It is also used to make kitchen glassware like casserole dishes which can be safely put in an oven to cook a meal. Figure 1.9 shows some common pieces of apparatus and diagrams used to represent them.

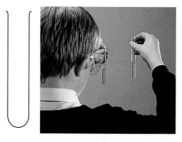

Test-tubes

Round bottomed flask

Flat bottomed flask

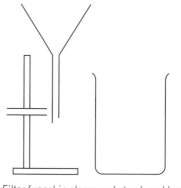

Separating funnel

Filter funnel in clamp and stand, and beaker

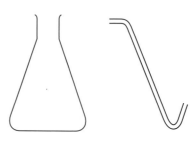

heat

Bunsen burner, tripod and gauze

Conical flask with delivery tube

**Figure 1.9**

# Bunsen burner

Robert Bunsen (1811–1899) was a German scientist. He made many investigations and his work included the invention of a battery and developing a way of identifying substances from the flames they produced. This method has been developed to identify substances in stars.

Bunsen is best known for the Bunsen burner, although he did not, in fact, invent it. However, he used it so widely in his investigations that other scientists began to use it too. Today it is used in laboratories throughout the world to give a strong steady source of heat without smoke.

By using the burner, Bunsen and a colleague discovered two new elements (see Table 4.1 page 49).

1 In what century did Bunsen live?
2 How old was he when he died?
3 Why is the burner named after him?
4 What are the advantages of using a burner, compared with a fire or a candle?
5 Who was Bunsen's colleague, and what were the elements they discovered?
6 How old was Bunsen when he discovered the new elements?

**Figure A**   Robert Bunsen.

When a record of an experiment is being made, a diagram of how the apparatus was set up is included. Each piece of apparatus can be represented diagrammatically so the way the apparatus was set up can be clearly seen.

7 What are the three pieces of apparatus represented by the diagrams in Figure 1.10?

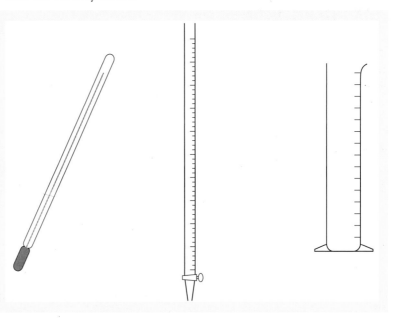

**Figure 1.10**

**8** Figure 1.11 shows how some pieces of apparatus were set up in an experiment. Draw a diagram of them and label each one.

**9** What is the volume of liquid in the measuring cylinder in Figure 1.12 a)?

**10** How would you measure 10 ml of liquid out of a full burette?

**11** How much liquid has been removed from the burette in Figure 1.12 b)?

**12** What is the volume of gas in the syringe in Figure 1.12 c)?

**13** What is the mass of the beaker on the balance in Figure 1.12 d)?

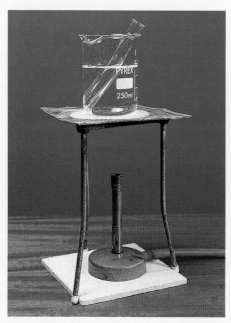

**Figure 1.11** Apparatus for a simple experiment.

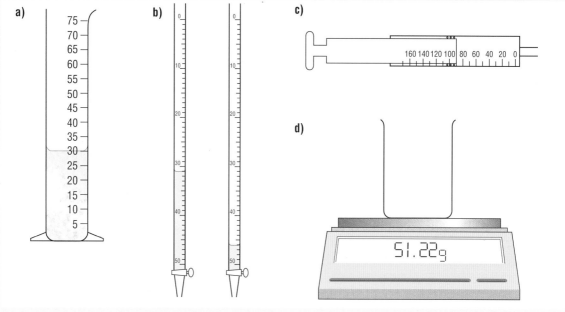

**Figure 1.12**

## More complicated apparatus

Some pieces of apparatus are complicated. For example, the Liebig condenser is used to convert steam into water. Figure 1.13 shows the Liebig condenser set up with other pieces of apparatus to carry out distillation (see also page 44). In this apparatus set-up, also note how bungs with tubes passing through them are represented diagrammatically. The condenser is named after Justus von Liebig (1803–1873), a famous chemist of the 19th Century.

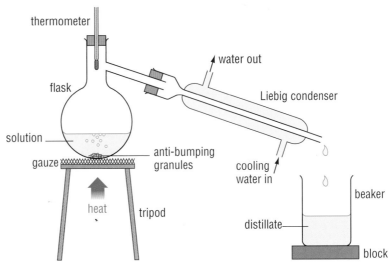

**Figure 1.13**  Apparatus for distillation with a Liebig condenser.

# Laboratory rules

Laboratories are busy places. There may be about 30 people doing investigations in a laboratory at the same time. They may be using gas, water, electricity, a wide range of glass apparatus and some hazardous chemicals. Despite the large amount of activity, there are fewer accidents in laboratories than in most other parts of a school. The reason for this is that when people work in laboratories, they generally take great care to follow the advice of the teacher and the rules on the laboratory wall.

Laboratory rules can be set out in many ways, but should cover the same good advice. Here is an example.

### Entering and leaving the laboratory
- Do not run into or out of the laboratory.
- Make sure that school bags are stored safely.
- Put stools under the bench when not in use.
- Leave the bench-top clean and dry.

### General behaviour

- Do not run in the laboratory
- Do not eat or drink in the laboratory.
- Work quietly.

### Preparing to do practical work

- Tie back long hair and if lab coats are available wear them, buttoned up.
- Wear safety spectacles when anything is to be heated or if any hazardous chemicals are to be used.

### During experiments

- Never point a test-tube containing chemicals at anyone, and do not examine the contents by looking down the tube.
- Tell your teacher about any breakage or spillage at once. If you are at all unsure of the practical work, check with your teacher that you are following the correct procedure.
- Only carry out investigations approved by your teacher, and use the gas, water and electricity supplies sensibly.

**Figure 1.14** Good laboratory practice.

**Figure 1.15**   Bad laboratory practice.

# What are they doing wrong?

Paul ran into the chemistry laboratory because he was keen to do an experiment. He did not see the stool that was sticking out from under the bench and fell over it. He grabbed hold of the bench to stop his fall but his fingers ran into a pool of liquid that had been left on the bench-top and his hand slid, lost its grip and he fell to the floor.

The rest of the class had sat down by the time Paul had picked himself up and put his bag down in the middle of the space between the benches. As Jenny came back from the teacher's bench with a lighted taper for her Bunsen burner, she stumbled against Paul's bag. Her long hair swayed forwards into the taper flame. She jerked her head back and only the tips of a few strands of hair were singed.

Brian had lit his Bunsen burner and was holding a test-tube of liquid over the flame. He was eager to look down the test-tube and brushed aside the safety spectacles that Andrew was holding out for him. The liquid boiled quickly; a few drops shot out of the test-tube and just missed Brian's face.

'Look at that!' he exclaimed, and pointed the test-tube at Paul so he could see too. Jane put down the apple that she was secretly eating to see what Brian and Paul were doing. When she picked it up again, she did not notice the dark, sticky substance clinging to it that had come from the bench-top. She quickly put her apple back into her bag, as the teacher approached to check her experiment.

*(continued)*

'Did Mrs Jones say to put the apparatus this way round or that way round?' asked Jenny, when the teacher had gone away.

'I don't know. I was too busy unsticking my apple from the bottom of my bag,' replied Jane. 'It looks all right like that. Light the Bunsen burner.'

'That's not right!' shouted Angela. Her loud voice made Brian jump and he dropped his test-tube. Mrs Jones looked round at Angela for a moment, but went off to stop Paul picking up the broken glass with his fingers.

'It should be like ours,' continued Angela in a quieter voice. 'Mrs Jones says it is OK.'

'But Paul's isn't like that,' cried Jenny.

'No,' whispered Paul. 'I'm making up my own experiment. If I light this paper in the sink and put this wire behind that dripping tap and just press this switch then . . .'

**1** List the things that the pupils are doing wrong in this story.

**2** What did the pupils who were in the laboratory before this class do wrong?

*For discussion*

**What are the reasons for each of the laboratory rules? What other rules could you add?**

**14** What do you understand by the words:

    **a)** corrosive,

    **b)** irritant,

    **c)** flammable,

    **d)** radioactive,

    **e)** toxic?

## Warning signs

Like all sciences, chemistry is a practical subject but some of the substances that are used are dangerous if not handled properly. The containers of these substances are labelled with a warning symbol such as these.

| corrosive | explosive | harmful or irritant | highly flammable | oxidising | radioactive | toxic |

**Figure 1.16** Warning symbols.

## From school laboratory to chemical plant

The laboratories in schools and colleges where chemistry is taught are called teaching laboratories. In these laboratories most of the apparatus is simple, like the pieces shown in Figure 1.9. Some apparatus used for advanced work may be more complicated and is fitted together by ground-glass joints (see Figure 1.17).

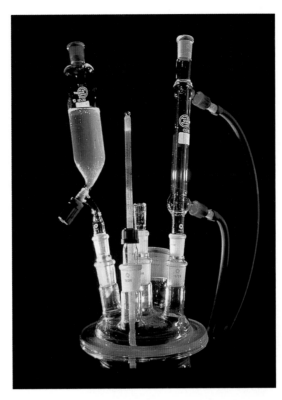

**Figure 1.17** Advanced chemical glassware connected by ground-glass joints.

The most complicated assemblies of apparatus are found in research laboratories where new chemical processes are investigated and new materials are developed (see Figure 1.18).

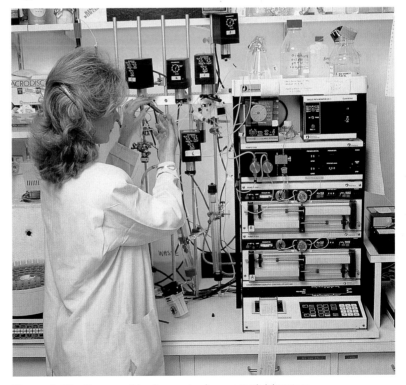

**Figure 1.18** The assembly of apparatus in a research laboratory.

Only small amounts of chemicals are used and made in the apparatus in research laboratories. Later, if it is thought that the process can be used to make large amounts of a material cheaply, a larger version of the apparatus is made and tested to see whether the process continues to work safely. If the larger version is found to be safe then a full-size version of the apparatus, now called a chemical plant, is built. Here, large amounts of chemicals are used to make large amounts of useful materials (see Figure 1.19).

**Figure 1.19**  A chemical plant that produces fertilisers.

# ◆ SUMMARY ◆

◇ Chemistry developed from alchemy about 200 years ago *(see page 1)*.
◇ Special apparatus is used to measure the volume, mass and temperature of a substance *(see page 2)*.
◇ Laboratory apparatus can be represented in diagrams *(see page 6)*.
◇ Rules need to be followed to be safe in investigations in the laboratory *(see page 9)*.
◇ Warning signs are used on the containers of dangerous substances *(see page 12)*.
◇ The work done in school laboratories can be applied in chemical research and the chemical industry *(see page 12)*.

## *End of chapter question*

**1** What advice can you give to someone to help them to:
   **a)** work safely in a chemical laboratory,
   **b)** take careful readings in experiments?

# 2 *The world of matter*

## Matter everywhere

**Figure 2.1**  School party hiking in the rain.

*For discussion*

Select one state of matter and imagine that it has been removed from the world. List things that could not exist if it was absent.

Do the same for the other two states of matter.

Would it be possible to live in any of the three imaginary worlds?

The three states of matter are solid, liquid and gas. When you go for a walk you move across the solid surface of the Earth. Your body pushes through a mixture of gases that we call the air. If it rains as you walk along, droplets of liquid fall from the sky. Solids, liquids and gases are the three states of matter on this planet, and for most other places in the Universe too (see page 54). Not only does your body move through a world made from the three states of matter, it is also made from the three states of matter. Solid bones are moved by solid muscles, while liquids move through your blood vessels and intestines. When you breathe in, air (a mixture of gases) fills your windpipe and lungs.

## Properties of matter

You can tell one state of matter from another by examining its properties.

Solids, liquids and gases all have mass and volume. They also have density, which is found by dividing the mass of the substance by its volume. For example, a solid with a mass of 100 g and a volume of 10 cm$^3$ has a density of $100/10 = 10 \, \text{g/cm}^3$. Another solid with a mass of 200 g and a volume of 10 cm$^3$ has a density of $200/10 = 20 \, \text{g/cm}^3$. This second solid has a higher density than the first solid.

1 Make a table of the properties of the three states of matter.

2 How are all three states of matter **a)** similar and **b)** different?

3 Calculate the densities of these substances:

   **a)** a plank of wood used for a shelf that has a volume of 1000 cm$^3$ and a mass of 650 g,

   **b)** the petrol in a car petrol tank that has a volume of 3000 cm$^3$ and a mass of 2400 g,

   **c)** the air in a box of 1000 cm$^3$ that has a mass of 1.3 g.

A solid has got a definite shape and a high density. It is very hard to make it flow or to compress (squash) it. A solid has a definite mass and a volume that does not change. A liquid also has a definite mass and volume. Its density is high and it is hard to compress, but it is easy to make it flow. The shape of the liquid varies and depends on the shape of the container holding it. The shape and volume of a gas vary, and it is easy to make it flow and to compress it. A gas has a definite mass but its density is low.

**Figure 2.2** A solid, a liquid and a gas.

## Using the properties of matter

The different properties of solids, liquids and gases lead to specific uses.

As solids have fixed shapes and volumes and are hard to compress, they are used to build structures that range in size from tiny machines to office tower blocks.

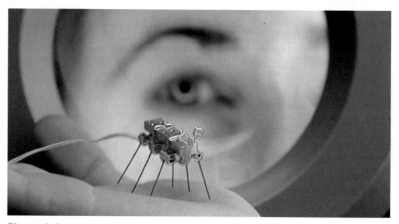

**Figure 2.3** A 'robot gnat' developed by nanotechnology.

**Figure 2.4** A tower block under construction in Canary Wharf, London.

In structures with moving parts, the solids rub against each other and are worn away. This wearing away is reduced by using a liquid – oil. The oil flows over the surfaces of the moving parts and forms a coating that also moves. This lets the different parts move over each other smoothly without rubbing.

A moving car is stopped by pressing the brake pedal with the right foot. Beneath the pedal is a cylinder, which is connected by pipes to four other cylinders—one by the brakes of each wheel. The cylinders and pipes are full of a liquid called brake fluid. When the pedal is pushed down, the force is applied to the liquid in the pipes and cylinders. As the liquid cannot be squashed,

**Figure 2.5** Oil is used in this engine to prevent wear.

it pushes outwards through levers to the brake pads on all four wheels at once. The pads rub against the wheels and slow them down. If the brakes did not work together the car would skid out of control.

**Figure 2.6** Droplet suspension as an aerosol is sprayed.

If a gas is squashed into a small space and is then released, it spreads out rapidly. A compressed gas is used in an aerosol spray to spread droplets of liquid. When the nozzle of the spray is pressed down, some of the gas is released, causing the liquid in the can to form droplets and spread out. The droplets may contain chemicals to kill flies or to give a pleasant smell to a room.

Air is a mixture of gases. To make a bicycle ride more comfortable, air is compressed into the bicycle tyres. Air is pumped into a tyre to give it strength, but as the tyre moves over the small bumps in the road, they push on the flexible tyre walls and squash some of the air even more. This stops the pushing force of the bumps being transferred to the bicycle and stops the cyclist from being shaken about.

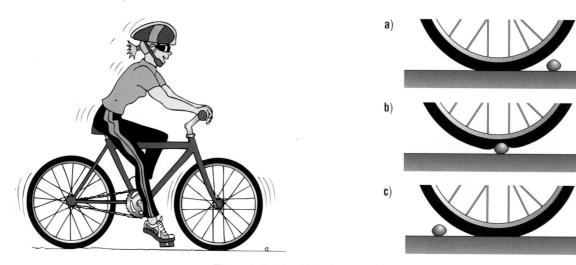

**Figure 2.7** A cyclist going over a bump.

# The first ideas about matter

The earliest people used the materials they could find around them such as wood, stone, antlers and skin. When people learned to make fire they began to change one material into another. First they learned how to cook food, then how to bake clay and make pottery and bricks. Eventually they learned how to heat some rocks in charcoal fires so strongly that a chemical reaction took place in which a metal was produced (see page 127).

By 600 BC, philosophers in the Greek civilisation were thinking about what different things were made of. They were puzzled by the way one substance could be changed into another. They asked the question, 'If a rock can be turned into metal, what really is the rock? Is the rock a kind of metal or is the metal a kind of rock?' They then thought that if one substance could change into another, perhaps it could go on changing into other substances. They did not carry out experiments to test their observations and ideas but tried to explain them with more ideas.

A Greek philosopher called Thales (642–546 BC) believed that all substances were made from different forms of one single substance. He called this substance an element. He observed how water changed from solid to liquid and gas and how plants and animals needed water to stay alive. From these observations he concluded that everything was made from different forms of water.

Other philosophers did not agree with Thales. Some believed that everything was made from air. They believed that air reached up from the ground and filled the whole of space. They thought that air could be squashed to make liquids and solids. Some philosophers suggested that fire was the basic element because it was always changing and it was this element in everything that made things change.

1 Why was the discovery of how to make fire important in making people think about the structure of materials?

2 Why were the Greeks' conclusions about matter not scientific?

3 In what ways do you think Thales saw water change?

4 If a substance was cold and dry, what element did the Greeks think it had?

5 What properties would a material have to show for the Greeks to decide that it contained fire?

6 Which elements do you think the Greeks thought were in:
   a) wood,
   b) oil,
   c) metal?
   Explain your answer.

7 How do you think they may have explained the changes they saw when a candle burned?

8 Why do you think the Greeks' idea of elements was used for such a long time?

*(continued)*

Eventually it was agreed that there were four elements from which all matter was made. The elements were water, air, fire and earth. Each element was given properties, and the way that the elements and their properties were related to each other is shown in Figure A.

The Greeks' ideas of the elements were used for 2000 years to explain the structure of materials and the way they change.

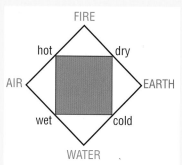

**Figure A**    The Greek elements.

**Figure B**    The four elements – air, water, earth and fire – can easily be identified in our surroundings.

# Changing states

The state of matter of a substance can be changed. It is changed by heating or cooling.

## Melting and freezing

If a solid is heated enough it loses its shape and starts to flow. This change is called melting and the solid turns into a liquid. The temperature at which melting takes place is called the melting point.

If a liquid is cooled enough it loses its ability to flow, forms a shape and turns into a solid. This change is called freezing. The temperature at which freezing takes place is called the freezing point. The temperature of the melting point is the same as the temperature of the freezing point.

## Evaporating and boiling

A solid turns into a liquid at one definite temperature but a liquid turns into a gas over a range of temperatures. For example, a drop of water can turn into a gas at room temperature of about 20°C while outside a puddle of water dries up in the warmth of the Sun. The process by which a liquid changes into a gas over a range of temperatures is called evaporation. The gas escapes from the surface of the liquid. If the temperature of the liquid is raised it evaporates faster. At a certain temperature the gas forms inside the liquid and makes bubbles which rise to the surface and burst into the air. This process is called boiling. The temperature at which it takes place is called the boiling point. If the boiling liquid is heated more strongly its temperature does not rise but it boils more quickly.

## Condensation

When a gas is cooled down it turns into a liquid by a process called condensation. This process is the opposite of evaporation. When the water in a kettle boils it forms a colourless gas called steam that rushes out of the kettle spout. A few centimetres above the spout the steam cools and condenses to form a cloud of water droplets which is often wrongly called steam. The real steam cannot be seen and is in the gap between the spout and the base of the cloud of water droplets.

**Figure 2.8**  A boiling kettle.

## Sublimation

There are a few solids which turn directly into a gas when they are heated. They do not change into a liquid first. This process is called sublimation.

Solid carbon dioxide, known as dry ice, sublimes when it is heated to $-78°C$. It can be used on a stage to produce a mist in the air when it warms up.

**Figure 2.9** Dry ice being used at a circus.

The term sublimation is also used when a gas turns directly into a solid. Sulphur vapour escaping from a volcano sublimes to form a solid crust on the rocks close by.

## Mass and the changes of state

When any substance changes state, such as turning from a liquid to a solid or a liquid to a gas, the mass of the substance does not change.

# The changing state of water

It has been estimated that there are 1.5 million million million litres of water on the Earth. Water can change from solid to liquid to gas and back to liquid and solid again at the temperatures found naturally on the Earth. Water moves between the oceans, atmosphere and land in a huge circular path called the water cycle (see Figure 2.10).

Water turns into a gas called water vapour by evaporation at any water surface. In the cool, upper air the water vapour condenses to form millions of water droplets that make the clouds. At the tops of the clouds it is so cold that the droplets freeze and form snowflakes. They fall through the cloud and melt to form raindrops. Falling water in the form of rain, snow or hail is called precipitation. Plant roots take up the water that passes through the soil, and their leaves return water to the atmosphere by transpiration.

**4** Water vapour can also condense on the ground at night. What is this condensation called? If this substance freezes we give it another name. What is it?

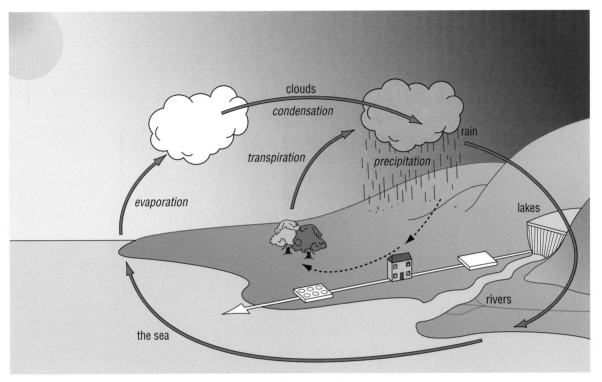

**Figure 2.10**   The water cycle.

5 Make a diagram to show the
states of matter and the
processes that change them.
Start by copying out Figure 2.11
then add the words evaporating,
melting, boiling, condensing,
subliming and freezing to the
appropriate arrows.

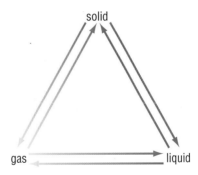

**Figure 2.11**   The interaction of states of matter.

# Particles of matter

Observations on the three states of matter and how they
change can be explained by considering that matter is
made of particles. This is called the 'particle theory of
matter'.

## Particles in the three states of matter

In solids, strong forces hold the particles together in a
three-dimensional structure. In many solids the particles
form an orderly arrangement called a lattice. The
particles in all solids move a little. They do not change
position but vibrate to and fro about one position.

**6** According to the particle theory, why do liquids flow but solids do not?

**7** How is the movement of particles in gases different from the movement of particles in liquids?

In liquids, the forces that hold the particles together are weaker than in solids. The particles in a liquid can change position by sliding over each other.

In gases, the forces of attraction between the particles are very small and the particles can move away from each other and travel in all directions. When they hit each other or the surface of their container they bounce and change direction.

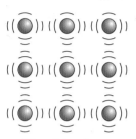

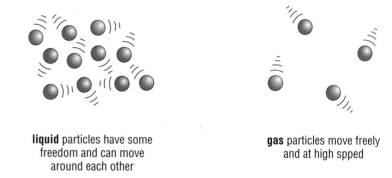

**solid** particles vibrate to and fro

**liquid** particles have some freedom and can move around each other

**gas** particles move freely and at high spped

**Figure 2.12** Arrangement of particles in a solid, liquid and gas.

# When matter changes state

## Expanding and melting

If a solid is heated, it expands and then melts. The heat provides the particles with more energy. The energy makes the particles vibrate more strongly and push each other a little further apart – the solid expands. If the solid is heated further, the energy makes the particles vibrate so strongly that they slide over each other and become a liquid. During the time from when the solid starts to melt until it has completely turned into a liquid its temperature does not rise. All the heat energy is used to separate the particles so that they can flow over one another.

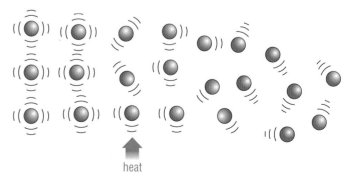

heat

**Figure 2.13** The particle arrangement in a solid changes as the heat turns it into a liquid.

# Freezing

If a liquid is cooled sufficiently the particles lose so much energy that they can no longer slide over each other. The only movement possible is the vibration to and fro about one position in the lattice. The liquid has become a solid.

**Figure 2.14**   The water on this waterfall has frozen to form ice.

# Evaporation

The particles in a liquid have different amounts of energy. The particles with the most energy move the

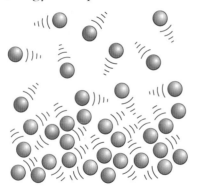

fastest. High energy liquid particles near the surface move so fast that they can break through the surface and escape into the air and form a gas.

**Figure 2.15**   Evaporation.

# Boiling

When a liquid is heated all the particles receive more energy and move more quickly. The fastest moving particles escape from the liquid surface or collect in the

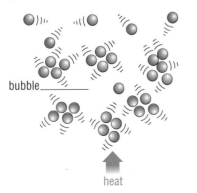

bubble

liquid to form bubbles. The bubbles rise to the surface and burst open into the air. The fast moving particles released from the liquid form a gas.

heat

**Figure 2.16**   Boiling.

## Condensation

The particles in a gas possess a large amount of energy which they use to move. If the particles are cooled they lose some of their energy and slow down. If the gas is cooled sufficiently, the particles lose so much energy that

they can no longer bounce off each other when they meet. The particles now slide over each other and form a liquid.

**Figure 2.17** Breathing onto a cold window causes water vapour in your breath to condense.

## Sublimation

When a few substances, such as iodine and solid carbon dioxide, are heated, the energy the particles receive makes them separate and form a gas without forming a liquid first. This is called sublimation.

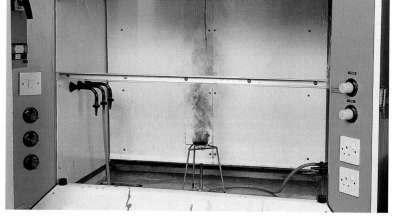

**8** How is melting different from evaporation?

**9** How is boiling different from sublimation?

**10** How are condensation and freezing similar?

**Figure 2.18** When solid iodine is heated it sublimes to form a gas. This is always done in a fume cupboard.

# Pressure

Solids can generate pressure – think of a brick pressing down on your toes. Liquids can generate pressure too. A dam has to be built with thick walls to withstand the pressure of the water that collects in the reservoir behind it.

A gas does not have a surface like a solid or a liquid but it still pushes on any surface with which it makes contact. This push on the surface area of a liquid or solid is called pressure.

A gas contains millions of quickly moving particles. Every second, large numbers are bouncing off the walls of the gas container. The force of these particles as they push against the surface gives rise to the gas pressure.

If the gas is heated the particles move faster and bounce off the container surface more frequently and with more force, so the gas pressure rises. When the gas is cooled the particles move more slowly. They bounce off the container's surface less frequently and with less force, and the gas pressure falls.

When a gas is squashed into a smaller volume but its temperature is kept the same, as shown in Figure 2.19, the particles have less space in which to move. They bounce off the container walls more frequently and the gas pressure rises.

**11** What two things can make the pressure of a gas rise?

**12 a)** What happens to the gas pressure if the gas is released from a small into a large container?

**b)** Why does the gas pressure change?

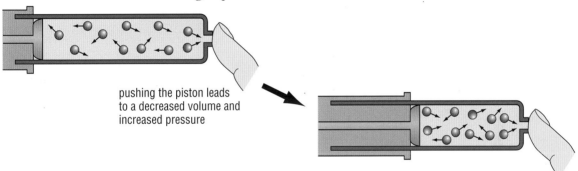

pushing the piston leads to a decreased volume and increased pressure

**Figure 2.19** Gas pressure can be explained using the particle theory.

## Pressure and changes of state

The state of matter of a substance can be changed by changing the pressure acting on it. Under very high pressure a gas can be turned into a liquid or a liquid into a solid.

### *Pressure on ice*

As skaters move across the ice their weight pushes down through the small surface of the blades and makes a large pressure. The ice beneath the blade melts. When the skaters have passed by, the pressure is reduced on the ice surface and the water there freezes again. This change happens because ice is less dense than its liquid form, water. The change does not happen with other solids because they are denser than the liquids they form when they melt.

## *On other planets*

The conditions on other planets in the Solar System are very different from conditions on Earth. Jupiter for example is made from a very large amount of hydrogen. The pressures and temperatures near the centre of the planet have made the hydrogen there into a solid like a metal. Above the solid hydrogen there is a vast ocean of liquid hydrogen.

Most of the planet Uranus is made from ammonia (the strong smelling gas that sometimes evaporates from a baby's nappy), methane (the gas used in cookers and fires) and water. The conditions near the centre of the planet have changed large amounts of these substances into solids and liquids.

**13** Compare the structure of these planets with that of the Earth (see Figure 8.2 on page 92).

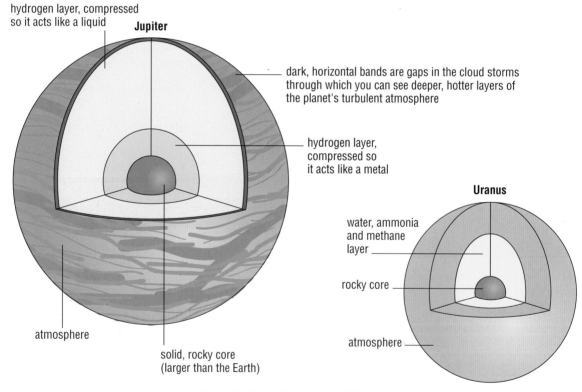

**Figure 2.20** Inside Jupiter and Uranus.

## Atmospheric pressure

The atmosphere is a mixture of gases that covers the surface of the Earth. The atmosphere is 1000 km thick and pushes on every square centimetre of the Earth's surface. The pressure of the atmosphere at sea level is called standard pressure and is about $10 \, N/cm^2$. It is the pressure at which the boiling point of any substance is measured. At the top of very high mountains the pressure of the atmosphere is less than at sea level.

## *Boiling and low pressure*

If a flask is connected to a vacuum pump and some of the air is sucked out there is less air inside the flask to push on the surfaces and the air pressure is smaller. The reduced air pressure allows evaporation to take place more quickly and less heat is needed to make the liquid boil. Lowering the atmospheric pressure on a liquid lowers the boiling point of the liquid.

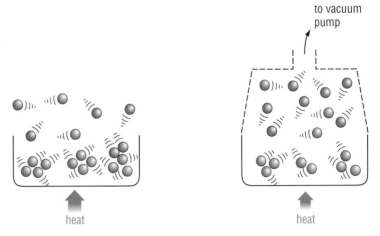

to vacuum pump

heat          heat

**14** If you boiled water at the top of a mountain, would you expect it to boil at 100°C? Explain your answer.

**Figure 2.21**   Lowering the pressure lowers the boiling point of a liquid.

## *Boiling and high pressure*

When a gas gets hot it expands and increases its pressure on the surfaces around it. If water is boiled in a pan with a lid, the steam escaping from the water pushes on the lid and makes it rise—allowing the gas to escape.

**Figure 2.22**   The lid on this pan of boiling water is being pushed up by the steam.

# Structure of matter

Democritus (about 470 BC–380 BC) was a Greek philosopher who thought about the structure of matter. He pondered on what would happen if you took a substance and divided it into two and then carried on dividing. He believed that eventually a tiny piece would be produced which could not be divided. He called this tiny piece of matter an atom. The word atom means indivisible.

Democritus believed in the four Greek elements (see page 20) and thought that each element was made from atoms that matched its properties. For example, he thought that the atoms of water were round and smooth so they could flow over each other. He also thought that fire was made of spiky atoms which inflicted the pain felt when skin is burned.

A Greek engineer called Hero lived about 400 years after Democritus but used his idea about atoms to explain his observations about air. He thought that the air was made of tiny particles with space between them. Hero believed this idea explained how air could be squashed. When air was squashed, particles moved closer together and had less space between them. Hero was unable to test his ideas because the Greeks at that time did not think that experiments had any importance.

Robert Boyle (1627–1691) performed experiments on gases. He was also the first person to write down the descriptions of his experiments very carefully so that other scientists could try them. Boyle found that there was a relationship between the pressure on a gas and its volume. For example, in one experiment he found that if the pressure on a gas was doubled, the volume of the gas halved. Boyle also believed that his observations could be explained by gases being made of atoms.

James Clerk Maxwell (1831–1879) and Ludwig Boltzmann (1844–1906) studied the results of experiments on gases and the idea of gases being made of atoms. They performed calculations and worked out the kinetic theory of gases in which they believed gases were made of tiny particles which could move rapidly in every direction. From this theory models were made of how particles moved in gases, liquids and solids.

1 Tear up a piece of paper as Democritus suggested. How small a paper particle can you make?

2 How might Democritus have described the shape of the atoms of the Greek element earth?

3 How does Hero's idea about air compare with the kinetic theory of gases (see page 27)?

4 How did the work of scientists like Boyle help Maxwell and Boltzmann?

5 Why was it logical to develop models about particles in solids and liquids from the kinetic theory of gases?

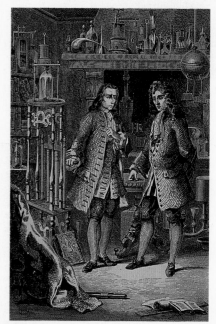

**Figure A**  Robert Boyle and his assistant at work in a laboratory.

# Diffusion

Diffusion is a process in which one substance spreads out through another. It occurs in liquids and gases. For example, if you put a drop of ink in a beaker of water the ink spreads out through the water by diffusion and colours it. The gases escaping from food cooking in the kitchen can move by diffusion to other rooms in the home. The moving particles in the different liquids flow over each other and the particles in the different gases bounce off each other. These movements in time spread all the particles of one substance evenly through the other. Liquids are denser than gases and this makes diffusion in liquids much slower than diffusion in gases.

15 Draw diagrams similar to those on pages 24 and 25 to show the following processes:
   a) sublimation,
   b) condensation,
   c) diffusion.

At start

After an hour

After a day

**Figure 2.23** Black ink diffusing through a beaker of water.

# Identifying substances

Every pure substance has a combination of melting point and boiling point that is different from those of other substances. These can then be used like a 'fingerprint' to identify the substance. Table 2.1 shows the melting and boiling points of some common substances.

**Table 2.1** Melting points and boiling points.

| Substance | Melting point °C | Boiling point °C |
|---|---|---|
| Nitrogen | −214 | −196 |
| Ammonia | −78 | −33 |
| Bromine | −7 | 59.1 |
| Mercury | −39 | 357 |
| Sodium chloride | 801 | 1420 |
| Iron | 1539 | 2887 |

16 Which substances are gases at:
   a) 0°C and b) 120°C?
17 Which substance is still solid at 1000°C?

## Testing for purity

If water contains other substances dissolved in it, the water is impure. The impure water forms ice that melts at a temperature below 0°C and boils at a temperature above 100°C. The melting and boiling points of a substance can therefore also be used to find out if a substance in the laboratory is pure.

## ◆ SUMMARY ◆

- There are three kinds or states of matter. They are solid, liquid and gas *(see page 15)*.
- Each state of matter has properties that are different from other states *(see page 15)*.
- The properties of matter have their uses *(see page 16)*.
- Matter can be changed from one state to another by the processes of melting, freezing, evaporation, boiling, condensation and sublimation *(see page 20)*.
- The particle theory of matter can be used to explain how matter behaves *(see page 23)*.
- The particles in the three states of matter behave differently *(see page 23)*.
- When the activity of the particles changes, matter changes from one state to another *(see page 24)*.
- Changes in gas pressure can be explained by the way the particles push on the sides of their container *(see page 26)*.
- The state of matter can be changed by changing the pressure acting on it *(see page 27)*.
- Diffusion is a process in which one substance spreads out through another *(see page 31)*.
- The combined melting point and boiling point of a substance can be used to identify it and to test its purity *(see page 31)*.

## *End of chapter questions*

1 How many different materials is your shoe made from? What are the properties of each material? How are these properties useful?
2 Use the particle theory of matter to explain what happens to the particles when an ice cube melts and the water it produces evaporates.
3 Why does a bicycle tyre get harder when you pump it up?

# 3 Separation of mixtures

## Mixtures and compounds

A mixture is composed of two or more separate substances. The composition of a mixture may vary widely. One mixture of two substances A and B might have a large amount of A and a small amount of B. Another mixture might have a small amount of A and a large amount of B. If A and B formed a chemical compound there would always be a fixed amount of each substance present.

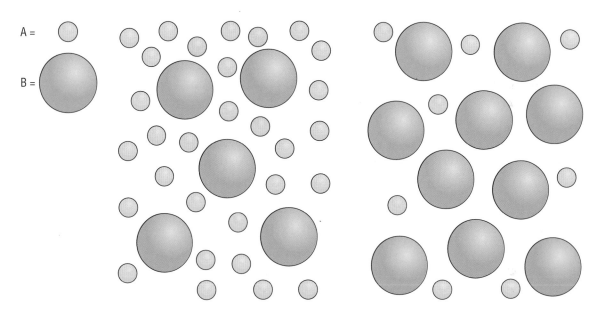

A =

B =

**Figure 3.1** Two different mixtures of A and B.

Compounds are formed during a chemical reaction and involve a change in heat energy (see Chapter 5). When a mixture is made there is no change in heat energy around the substances that are mixing. The substances in a mixture retain their individual properties. When the substances form a chemical compound they no longer retain their properties. The compound has its own properties.

The substances in a mixture can be separated by physically removing one substance from another, as shown in the separating techniques in this chapter. The substances which make up compounds cannot be separated physically. One or more chemical reactions may be needed to separate the substances in a chemical compound.

**1** Make a table to show the differences between mixtures and compounds.

# Different kinds of mixtures

## Solid/solid mixtures

Soil is a mixture of different solid particles. Some particles such as clay are very small while others such as sand are larger.

**Figure 3.2**  A cross-section of soil.

## Solid/liquid mixtures

If clay is stirred with water it forms a cloudy mixture. The tiny clay particles are suspended in the water. The mixture is called a suspension. If a solid dissolves in a liquid a solution is made (see page 35).

## Solid/gas mixtures

The smoke rising in the hot air from a bonfire contains particles of soot and ash. A mixture of solid and gas also occurs in the dust produced when the wall of a building is being cleaned by blasting a jet of sand at it.

## Liquid/liquid mixtures

Milk is a mixture of tiny droplets of fatty oil in water. This kind of mixture is called an emulsion. An emulsion mixture is also found in some kinds of paint.

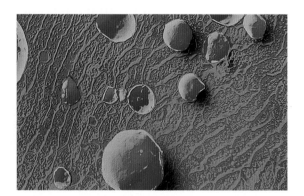

**Figure 3.3**  Fat globules in whole milk, as seen under a high power microscope.

## Liquid/gas mixtures

When water vapour in the air condenses above the cool surface of a lake or a field, the tiny droplets form a mist or fog.

When you press the top of an aerosol can, a mist of liquid droplets in a gas is sprayed into the air.

## Gas/liquid mixtures

When bubbles of gas are trapped in a liquid they form a foam. Foam is made when the nozzle of a shaving foam cylinder is pressed. Some products that protect you from sunburn are foams.

# Solutions

The most common form of a mixture in chemical experiments is the solution. A solution is made when a substance, called a solute, mixes with a liquid, called a solvent, in such a way that the solute can no longer be seen. This type of mixing is called dissolving.

Although the solute cannot be seen it has not taken part in a chemical reaction and can be recovered from the solution by separating it from the solvent. The solute may be a solid, liquid or gas.

**2** What is the difference between a solvent and a solute?

Copper sulphate dissolves in water to form a blue solution

Clay does not dissolve in water, but forms a suspension that settles to the bottom after some time

**Figure 3.4** Soluble and insoluble compounds.

**3** What is the difference between a substance that is soluble in water and one that is insoluble in water?

**4** What is the difference between an immiscible substance and an emulsion?

A liquid that dissolves in a solvent, water, for example, is said to be miscible with water. A liquid that does not dissolve in a solvent is said to be immiscible with it.

A gas or a solid that dissolves in a solvent is said to be soluble in that solvent. A solid or gas that does not dissolve in a solvent is said to be insoluble in that solvent (see Figure 3.4).

## Saturated solutions

If the temperature of a solvent is kept steady or constant, and the solute is added in small amounts, there comes a time when no more solute will dissolve. The solution is then said to be saturated. If the temperature of the saturated solution is raised, it is able to take in more solute until it becomes saturated at the new temperature.

## Solubility

The solubility of a solute in a solvent at a particular temperature is the maximum mass of the solute that will dissolve in 100 g of the solvent, before the solution becomes saturated.

If the temperature of the solvent is raised the solubility of the solute usually increases (see Figure 3.5). If the solubilities of a substance at different temperatures of the solvent are plotted on a graph, a solubility curve is made.

**5** What do the solubility curves of the three substances in Figure 3.5 show?

**6** How does the solubility of potassium nitrate change when the temperature of the solvent is raised from 30 to 50°C?

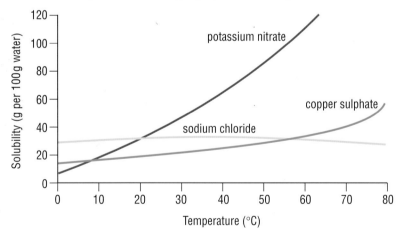

**Figure 3.5** Solubility curves.

## Liquids and gases in solvents

The miscibility of a liquid with a solvent may change with a change in temperature of the solvent. For example, ethanol and cyclohexane, which is used to make paint remover, form two separate layers when they are cold but become miscible when they are hot.

**7** How does the solubility of oxygen in water vary with the temperature of the water?

More gas will dissolve in cold water than in warm water – this is the opposite of what happens with solids. Hot water entering a river from a power station can warm the river water so much that not enough oxygen can dissolve in it for the fish to breathe. Some species of water animals can only live where there is a high concentration of oxygen in the water. These species must live in the cool waters of mountain streams.

## Different solvents

Water has been called the universal solvent because so many different substances dissolve in it. However, there are many liquids used as solvents in a wide range of products. Ethanol is used in perfumes, aftershaves and glues. Propanone is used to remove nail varnish and grease. Gloss paint is dissolved in white spirit.

Substances that dissolve in one solvent do not necessarily dissolve in others. Salt dissolves in water but not in ethanol. White sugar dissolves in both.

# Separating mixtures

The substances in a mixture have not taken part in a chemical reaction and have kept their original characteristics. These characteristics are used in the following techniques to separate the substances.

## Separating a solid/solid mixture

A mixture of two solids with particles of different sizes may be separated by using a sieve. The particles in soil are analysed by putting the soil in the top compartment of a soil sieve and shaking it. Each part of the soil sieve has a mesh with smaller holes than the one before. Different sized particles are caught in each layer as the soil moves from the top to the bottom.

Magnetic materials can be separated from non-magnetic materials by passing the materials close to a magnet. In a metal separator, the cylinder is a magnet that attracts iron and steel items to it, while other metals fall away. The magnetic materials are then knocked off the cylinder into another collection bay, as shown in Figure 3.7.

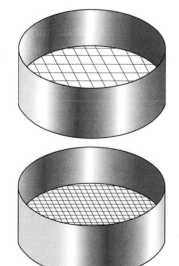

**Figure 3.6** A soil sieve.

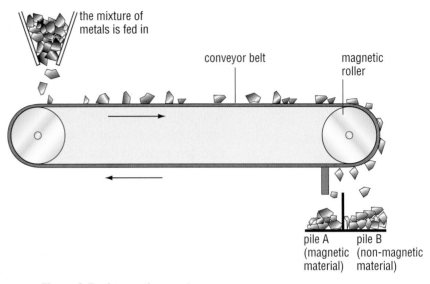

**Figure 3.7**  A magnetic separator.

Many metals are found in rocks combined with other substances and with a great deal of worthless material. This mixture is known as an ore (see page 120).

Metal compounds and the worthless material can be separated using a flotation cell. The ore is broken up into fragments and added to a mixture of water, oil and a range of chemicals. When compressed air is blown through the chemical mixture, a froth is produced which rises to the surface. The chemicals also help the particles containing the metal to cling to the froth, while the worthless material is left behind. The skimmers at the surface remove the froth and valuable metal compound.

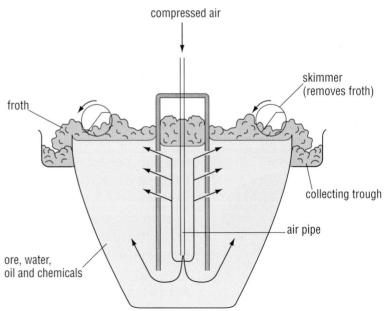

**8**  What is used in a flotation cell to separate a metal compound out of its ore?

**Figure 3.8**  A flotation cell.

## Separating an insoluble solid/liquid mixture

In the home, sieves are used to separate insoluble solids, such as peas, from liquids. This is possible because the particle size of the solid is very much larger than that of water. In chemistry, this is not usually the case and other methods are needed.

### *Large particles*

#### Decanting

Large particles of an insoluble solid in a liquid settle at the bottom of the liquid's container. They form a layer called a sediment. The liquid and solid can be separated by decanting. A liquid is decanted by carefully pouring it out of the container without disturbing the sediment at the bottom. At home, some medicines and sunburn lotions form a sediment in the bottom of the bottle and have to be shaken to mix the solid and liquid before being used.

**Figure 3.9**   Decanting a liquid from a jug.

### *Small particles*

#### Filtration

In many laboratory experiments, filtration is carried out by folding a filter paper to make a cone and inserting it in a filter funnel. The funnel is then supported above a collecting vessel and the mixture to be separated is poured into the funnel.

The filter paper is made of a mesh of fibres. It works like a sieve but the holes between the fibres are so small that only liquid can pass through them. The solid particles are left behind on the paper fibres.

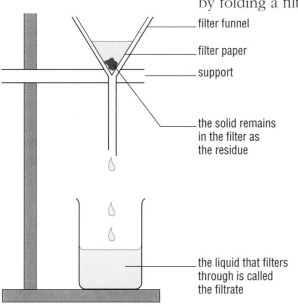

filter funnel

filter paper

support

the solid remains in the filter as the residue

the liquid that filters through is called the filtrate

**Figure 3.10**   Filtration with a filter funnel.

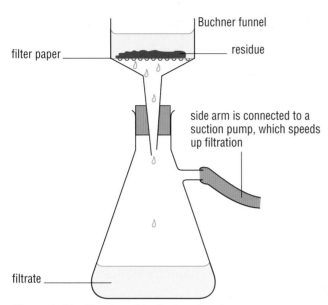

filter paper

Buchner funnel

residue

side arm is connected to a suction pump, which speeds up filtration

filtrate

**Figure 3.11** Filtration with a Buchner funnel.

## A fast filter

A Buchner funnel has holes in it. A filter paper is spread out over the holes. The funnel is fastened into the top of a flask which is connected to a suction pump by a rubber tube. The suction pump draws air out of the flask. When the mixture is poured into the funnel and the suction pump is switched on the air pressure inside the flask is reduced. The higher air pressure above the mixture pushes on it and speeds up filtration.

In both kinds of filtration the substance left behind in the filter paper is called the residue and the liquid that has passed through the filter paper is called the filtrate.

## Centrifuge

Very small insoluble particles in a liquid may be separated from it using a centrifuge. This machine has an electric motor which spins several test-tubes mounted on a central shaft. All the test-tubes are carefully balanced by having the same amount of liquid poured into them. As the test-tubes spin, the small particles are forced to the bottom and form a layer like a sediment. When the test-tubes are removed from the centrifuge the liquid can be decanted from them.

**9** What method of separation would you use for:
  **a)** water and fine sand,
  **b)** water and gravel,
  **c)** water with very tiny particles floating in it?
  In each case explain how the method of separation works.

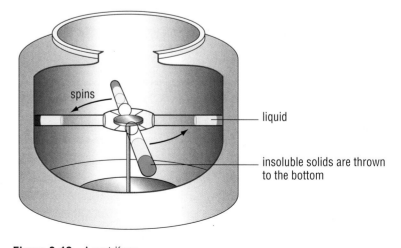

spins

liquid

insoluble solids are thrown to the bottom

**Figure 3.12** A centrifuge.

# Separating a solute from a solute/solvent mixture

These methods can be used to separate a solid solute from a solvent.

## *Evaporation*

If a solution is heated gently, the solvent evaporates from the surface until only the solid is left behind. Distilled water is made by boiling and condensing water (see page 43) to remove impurities.

**Figure 3.13** Copper sulphate solution being evaporated over a water bath.

Tap water and sea water may be compared with it by setting up samples of all three kinds of water and heating them gently until all the liquid has evaporated, leaving just any solid content.

## *Crystallisation*

A crystal is a solid structure with flat sides. Many substances form crystals. One way of making crystals is to start with a concentrated solution of a substance.

As the solution is gently heated the solvent evaporates and the concentration of the solute in the solution rises until the solution is saturated (see page 36). If the heat is removed at this time and the saturated solution is left to cool, the solid will form crystals.

**Figure 3.14** Crystals of copper sulphate formed in an evaporating dish.

## Separating several different solutes from a solvent - chromatography

A simple chromatography experiment can be performed with filter paper, a dropper, ink and water. A drop of ink is placed in the centre of the filter paper, then a drop of water is placed on top of it. The water dissolves the coloured pigments and spreads out through the filter paper, carrying the pigments with it. Each kind of pigment moves at a different speed to the others so that they spread out into different regions of the paper. When the separation is complete, the paper is dried. The paper with its separate pigments is called a chromatogram.

**10** The unknown mixture used in Figure 3.15 is suspected of containing substances A, B and C. Do the results confirm this?

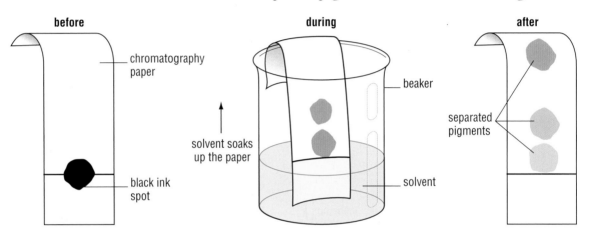

**Figure 3.15**   Simple paper chromatography.

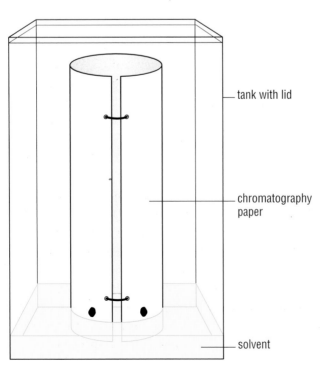

Substances that do not dissolve in water can be separated by chromatography by using other solvents, such as propanone. When one of these solvents is used the chromatography paper is enclosed in a tank. This makes sure that the solvent vapour does not escape but surrounds the paper keeping it saturated with solvent and helps the substances to separate.

**Figure 3.16**   A chromatography tank.

# Separating a solvent from a solute/solvent mixture

During evaporation or boiling, the liquid solvent is lost to the air. If the solvent is important it can be separated from the mixture using a process called distillation.

In a very simple form of distillation, the solution is placed in a test-tube which is set up as shown in Figure 3.17.

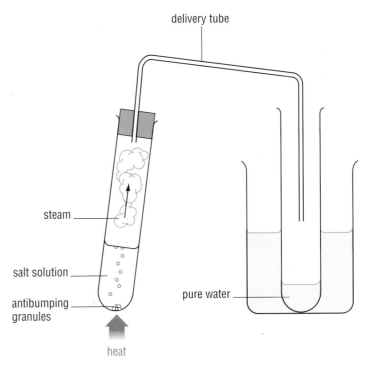

**Figure 3.17**  Simple distillation.

The antibumping granules provide many places where bubbles of gas may form as the water boils. The bubbles are small and steadily rise to the liquid surface where they burst. Without the granules, fewer but larger bubbles form that rise and burst with such force that they shake the test-tube.

As the water boils the steam moves along the delivery tube. At first the tube is cool enough to make some of the steam condense but as more steam passes along the tube it becomes hotter and no more condensation takes place. The cold water in the beaker keeps the walls of the second test-tube cool so that most of the steam condenses there and water collects at the bottom of the tube. The solid solute remains in the first tube. (Liquid and gas solutes are separated by fractional distillation.) The purity of the water can be checked by boiling it and recording its boiling point with a thermometer (see page 32).

### Distillation with a Liebig condenser

The Liebig condenser is a glass tube surrounded by a glass chamber called a water jacket. During the distillation process, water is allowed to flow from the cold tap through the water jacket and down the sink. The water takes away the heat from the hot vapour in the tube of the condenser and causes condensation. The liquid formed by the condensed vapour is called the distillate. It flows down the tube and drips into the collection flask.

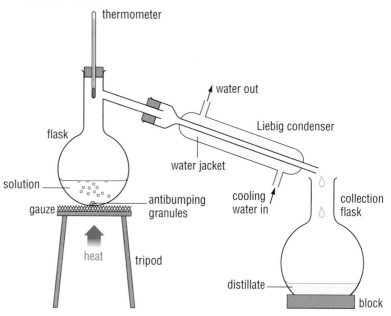

**Figure 3.18**  Distillation with a Liebig condenser.

**11**  Why is the Liebig condenser more efficient than the simple distillation apparatus?

## Separating two miscible liquids

### Fractional distillation

Two liquids with quite different boiling points, such as water (100°C) and ethanol (78°C), can be separated by fractional distillation.

The separation occurs in the fractionating column. This is filled with glass beads that provide a large surface area. During the fractionating process the liquids condense and evaporate from the surface many times. At first, in the lower part of the column, the water and ethanol vapours condense together on the cold beads. They warm them up and some of the ethanol and a little water vapour evaporate and move up a little further, then condense. As the solution continues to boil, this process of condensation and evaporation is repeated all the way up the column. Each time, more of the liquid with the lower boiling point – the ethanol – rises further, until it reaches the top. The ethanol vapour then passes down the Liebig condenser and is collected in the beaker. As the vapour passes the thermometer, a temperature of 78°C is recorded. This is the temperature at which pure ethanol boils. When most of the ethanol has passed the thermometer the temperature starts to rise. At this point, the process is stopped as the liquid in the flask is nearly all water.

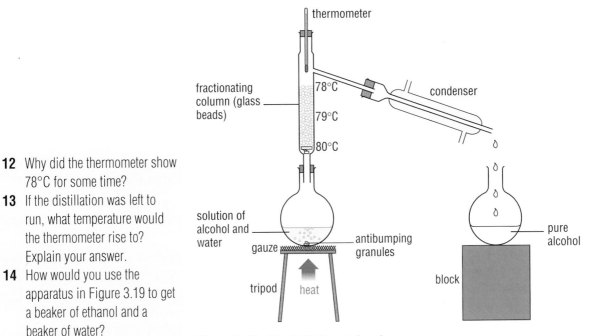

**12** Why did the thermometer show 78°C for some time?

**13** If the distillation was left to run, what temperature would the thermometer rise to? Explain your answer.

**14** How would you use the apparatus in Figure 3.19 to get a beaker of ethanol and a beaker of water?

**Figure 3.19**  The distillation of ethanol.

## Separating immiscible liquids

When two immiscible liquids are mixed together they eventually form layers, if left to stand. This can be seen when oil and vinegar are mixed together to form salad dressing.

**Figure 3.20**  Salad dressing mixture after shaking (left) and after standing for 10 minutes (right).

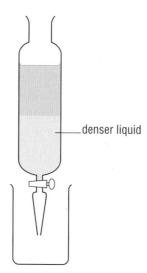

denser liquid

The less dense liquid forms a layer above the more dense liquid. The separating funnel (see Figure 3.21) can be used to separate them. The tap is opened to let the liquid in the lower layer flow away into a beaker. A second beaker can be used to collect the liquid from the upper layer.

**Figure 3.21**   A separating funnel.

# ◆ SUMMARY ◆

- A mixture is composed of two or more substances. There are no fixed amounts in which they combine. They can be separated by physically removing one substance from the other *(see page 33)*.
- There is a wide range of mixtures in which solids, liquids and gases combine together *(see page 34)*.
- A solution is composed of a solute and a solvent *(see page 35)*.
- When no more solute will dissolve in a solvent, the solution is said to be saturated *(see page 36)*.
- The maximum mass of solute that will dissolve in 100 g of solvent, at a particular temperature, is known as the solubility of the substance at that temperature *(see page 36)*.
- More gas will dissolve in cold water than in warm water *(see page 37)*.
- There are many solvents. Substances that dissolve in one solvent may not dissolve in others *(see page 37)*.
- Solids may be separated from each other with a sieve, magnetic separator or flotation cell *(see page 37)*.
- Solids may be separated from liquids by decanting, filtration or by using a centrifuge *(see page 39)*.
- A solid solute may be separated from a solvent by evaporation, crystallisation or chromatography *(see page 41)*.
- A solvent may be separated from a solid solute by distillation *(see page 43)*.
- Miscible liquids can be separated by fractional distillation *(see page 44)*.
- Two immiscible liquids can be separated by a separating funnel *(see page 45)*.

## *End of chapter question*

1  How would you separate the different parts of a mixture of sand and salty water?

# 4 Elements and atoms

## Elements and compounds

One of the main activities in chemistry is breaking down substances to discover what they are made of. During the course of this work chemists have discovered that some substances will not break down into simpler substances. These substances are called elements.

### Changing the idea of elements

Robert Boyle's experiments (see page 30) led him to believe that the Greeks' ideas about everything being made from four elements were wrong. He thought that elements could be identified by performing experiments. Any substance that could not be broken down into simpler substances in an investigation was an element. He also believed that two elements could be joined together to make a compound and that they could be split apart again.

Some other scientists disagreed with Boyle. They observed that when water was heated for many days, a sediment was produced. They believed this supported the Greeks' ideas about elements because it showed that the element water was being turned into the element earth.

Antoine Lavoisier (1743–1794) performed an experiment in which water was boiled and condensed in a piece of apparatus called a pelican (see Figure A) for 101 days. At the end of this time he found that the weight of water remained unchanged, but the weight of the sediment was equal to the weight of material lost by the pelican. Lavoisier added his support to Boyle's ideas and produced a list of substances that he considered to be elements. In his list were 21 elements we recognise today such as hydrogen, nickel and zinc. Lavoisier's work encouraged other chemists to search for elements.

1 How did Boyle believe that elements could be found?
2 How did Lavoisier show that water did not turn into a sediment?
3 What important process did Lavoisier use to find the amounts of substances in his experiment?

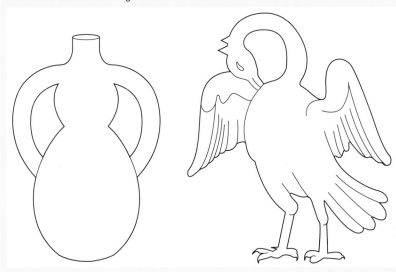

**Figure A**   Lavoisier's condensing apparatus was called a pelican due to its bird-like shape.

**1** How many elements were discovered in
  **a)** the 17th Century,
  **b)** the 18th Century,
  **c)** the 19th Century?
**2** Which three scientists discovered the most elements?
**3** How many Swedish scientists discovered new elements?
**4** Which UK scientist discovered the most elements?

# Discovery of the elements

Before 1669 the following elements had already been discovered – carbon, sulphur, iron, copper, arsenic, silver, tin, antimony, gold, mercury and lead. Some had been known for thousands of years, although they had not been recognised as elements. The order in which the other elements were discovered is shown in Table 4.1. This table uses mainly European historical data but it is known that the Chinese also practised alchemy, so some of the elements could have been discovered by them at an earlier date.

**Table 4.1** The discovery of the elements.

| Date | Element | Discoverer | Brief description |
|---|---|---|---|
| 1669 | Phosphorus | H. Brand (Germany) | white, red, black solid |
| 1737 | Cobalt | G. Brandt (Sweden) | reddish metal |
| 1746 | Zinc | A.S. Marggraf (Germany) | blue–white metal |
| 1748 | Platinum | A. de Ulloa (Spain) | blue–white metal |
| 1751 | Nickel | A.F. Cronstedt (Sweden) | silver–white metal |
| 1753 | Bismuth | C.F. Geoffroy (France) | silver–red metal |
| 1766 | Hydrogen | H. Cavendish (UK) | colourless gas |
| 1771–1774 | Oxygen | C.W. Scheele (Sweden) J. Priestley (UK) | colourless gas |
| 1772 | Nitrogen | D. Rutherford (UK) | colourless gas |
| 1774 | Chlorine | C.W. Scheele (Sweden) | green–yellow gas |
| 1774 | Manganese | J.G. Gahn (Sweden) | red–white metal |
| 1781 | Molybdenum | P.J. Hjelm (Sweden) | silver–grey metal |
| 1783 | Tellurium | F.J. Muller (Austria) | silver–grey solid |
| 1783 | Tungsten | J.J. de Elhuya, F. de Elhuya (Spain) | grey metal |
| 1789 | Zirconium | M.H. Klaproth (Germany) | shiny, white metal |
| 1789 | Uranium | M.H. Klaproth (Germany) | blue–white metal |
| 1794 | Yttrium | J. Gadolin (Finland) | shiny, grey metal |
| 1795 | Titanium | M.H. Klaproth (Germany) | silvery metal |
| 1798 | Beryllium | N-L Vauquelin (France) | brown powder |
| 1798 | Chromium | N-L Vauquelin (France) | silvery metal |
| 1801 | Niobium | C. Hatchett (UK) | grey metal |
| 1802 | Tantalum | A.G. Ekeberg (Sweden) | silvery metal |
| 1803 | Cerium | J.J. Berzelius, W. Hisinger (Sweden) M.H. Klaproth (Germany) | grey metal |

*(continued)*

| Date | Element | Discoverer | Brief description |
|------|---------|-----------|-------------------|
| 1803 | Palladium | W.H. Wollaston (UK) | silver–white metal |
| 1804 | Rhodium | W.H. Wollaston (UK) | grey–blue metal |
| 1804 | Osmium | S. Tennant (UK) | blue–grey metal |
| 1804 | Iridium | S. Tennant (UK) | silver–white metal |
| 1807 | Potassium | H. Davy (UK) | silver–white metal |
| 1807 | Sodium | H. Davy (UK) | silver–white metal |
| 1808 | Magnesium | H. Davy (UK) | silver–white metal |
| 1808 | Calcium | H. Davy (UK) | silver–white metal |
| 1808 | Strontium | H. Davy (UK) | silver–white metal |
| 1808 | Barium | H. Davy (UK) | silver–white metal |
| 1811 | Iodine | B. Courtois (France) | grey–black solid |
| 1817 | Lithium | J.A. Arfwedson (Sweden) | silver–white metal |
| 1817 | Cadmium | F. Stromeyer (Germany) | blue–white metal |
| 1818 | Selenium | J.J. Berzelius (Sweden) | grey solid |
| 1824 | Silicon | J.J. Berzelius (Sweden) | grey solid |
| 1825–1827 | Aluminium | H.C. Oersted (Denmark)<br>F. Wohler (Germany) | silver–white metal |
| 1826 | Bromine | A.J. Balard (France) | red–brown liquid |
| 1829 | Thorium | J.J. Berzelius (Sweden) | grey metal |
| 1830 | Vanadium | N.G. Sefstrom (Sweden) | silver–grey metal |
| 1839 | Lanthanum | C.G. Mosander (Sweden) | metallic solid |
| 1843 | Terbium | C.G. Mosander (Sweden) | silvery metal |
| 1843 | Erbium | C.G. Mosander (Sweden) | silver–grey metal |
| 1844 | Ruthenium | K.K. Klaus (Estonia) | blue–white metal |
| 1860 | Caesium | R.W. Bunsen, G.R. Kirchhoff (Germany) | silver–white metal |
| 1861 | Rubidium | R.W. Bunsen, G.R. Kirchhoff (Germany) | silver–white metal |
| 1861 | Thallium | W. Crookes (UK) | blue–grey metal |
| 1863 | Indium | F. Reich, H.T. Richter (Germany) | blue–silver metal |
| 1868 | Helium | J.N. Lockyer (UK) | colourless gas |
| 1875 | Gallium | L. de Boisbaudran (France) | grey metal |
| 1878 | Ytterbium | J-C-G de Marignac (Switzerland) | silvery metal |
| 1878–1879 | Holmium | J.L. Soret (France)<br>P.T. Cleve (Sweden) | silvery metal |
| 1879 | Scandium | L.F. Nilson (Sweden) | metallic solid |
| 1879 | Samarium | L. de Boisbaudran (France) | light grey metal |

*(continued)*

| Date | Element | Discoverer | Brief description |
|------|---------|------------|-------------------|
| 1879 | Thulium | P.T. Cleve (Sweden) | metallic solid |
| 1880 | Gadolinium | J-C-G de Marignac (Switzerland) | silver–white metal |
| 1885 | Neodymium | C. Auer von Welsbach (Austria) | yellow–white metal |
| 1885 | Praseodymium | C. Auer von Welsbach (Austria) | silver–white metal |
| 1886 | Dysprosium | L. de Boisbaudran (France) | metallic solid |
| 1886 | Fluorine | H. Moissan (France) | green–yellow gas |
| 1886 | Germanium | C.A. Winkler (Germany) | grey–white metal |
| 1894 | Argon | W. Ramsay, Lord Rayleigh (UK) | colourless gas |
| 1898 | Krypton | W. Ramsay, M.W. Travers (UK) | colourless gas |
| 1898 | Neon | W, Ramsay, M. W. Travers (UK) | colourless gas |
| 1898 | Polonium | Mme M.S. Curie (Poland/France) | metallic solid |
| 1898 | Xenon | W. Ramsay, M.W. Travers (UK) | colourless gas |
| 1898 | Radium | P. Curie (France), Mme M.S. Curie (Poland/France), M.G. Bermont (France) | silvery metal |
| 1899 | Actinium | A. Debierne (France) | metallic solid |
| 1900 | Radon | F.E. Dorn (Germany) | colourless gas |
| 1901 | Europium | E.A. Demarçay (France) | grey metal |
| 1907 | Lutetium | G. Urbain (France) | metallic solid |
| 1917 | Protactinium | O. Hahn (Germany), Fr L. Meitner (Austria), F. Soddy, J.A. Cranston (UK) | silvery metal |
| 1923 | Hafnium | D. Coster (Netherlands) G.C. de Hevesy (Hungary/Sweden) | grey metal |
| 1925 | Rhenium | W. Noddack, Fr I. Tacke, O. Berg (Germany) | white–grey metal |
| 1937 | Technetium | C. Perrier (France) E. Segre (Italy/USA) | silver–grey metal |
| 1939 | Francium | Mlle M. Percy (France) | metallic solid |
| 1940 | Astatine | D.R. Corson, K.R. Mackenzie (USA) E. Segre (Italy/USA) | metallic solid |
| 1945 | Promethium | J. Marinsky, L.E. Glendenin, C.O Corgell (USA) | metallic solid |

## Properties of elements and compounds

Only a very few of the substances you see around you are elements. The most common solid elements are metals such as aluminium and copper, though objects made of the elements gold and silver may be more obvious.

**Figure 4.1** Mercury and bromine are liquid at room temperature.

There are only two elements that are liquid at room temperature and standard pressure. They are mercury and bromine. Eleven elements are gases under normal conditions. Oxygen and nitrogen, which together form about 98% of the air, are two of them.

Each element has its own special properties. For example, sodium is a soft, silvery-white metal with a melting point of 97.86°C and a boiling point of 884°C and chlorine is a yellow–green gas with a melting point of −100.97 °C and a boiling point of −34.03 °C.

Most substances are made from two or more elements that are joined together. These substances are called compounds. They have properties which are different from the elements that make them. Common salt, for example, is a compound of sodium and chlorine and is a white solid with a melting point of 801 °C and a boiling point of 1420 °C. It easily forms crystals.

# Dalton's atomic theory

John Dalton (1766–1844) studied the work of Democritus (see page 30), Lavoisier and Proust. Antoine Lavoisier investigated the changes that took place when two chemicals reacted and formed a new compound. He weighed the chemicals before the reaction and then weighed the compound that was formed. Lavoisier found that the total mass of the chemicals was the same as the mass of the compound that was produced. From this result and from the results of similar experiments, Lavoisier set out his law of conservation of mass which stated that matter is neither created nor destroyed during a chemical reaction.

**Figure A** John Dalton.

*(continued)*

Joseph Proust (1754–1826) followed Lavoisier's example by carefully weighing the chemicals in his experiments. He discovered that when he broke up copper carbonate into its elements of copper, carbon and oxygen and then weighed them, they always combined in the same proportions of 5.3 parts of copper, 4 parts of oxygen and one part of carbon. He found that other substances were made from different proportions of elements and these proportions were always the same too, no matter how large or small the amounts of elements that were used. From his work, Proust devised the law of definite proportions which stated that the elements in a compound are always present in a certain definite proportion, no matter how the compound is made.

John Dalton put together his atomic theory and suggested that:

- All matter is composed of tiny particles called atoms.
- Atoms cannot be divided up into smaller particles and cannot be destroyed.
- Atoms of an element all have the same mass and properties.
- The atoms of different elements have different masses and different properties.
- Atoms combine in simple whole numbers when they form compounds.

This theory helped chemists at the time, but the results of later investigations showed that it was not completely correct.

1 Which parts of the theory come from:
   a) Democritus's idea (see page 30),
   b) Lavoisier's work?
2 Why do a block of copper and a similarly sized block of carbon not weigh the same?
3 Whose work led to the statement that atoms combine in simple whole numbers?
4 You can return to this theory later when you have read other parts of this chapter and identify the parts that we now know are not correct.

# Atoms

Each element is made of atoms. An atom is about a ten-millionth of a millimetre across. It is made of sub-atomic particles. At the centre of the atom is the nucleus. It is made from two kinds of sub-atomic particles called protons and neutrons. (Hydrogen is an exception because it has only a proton in its nucleus.) A proton has the same mass as a neutron. It also has a positive electrical charge, while the neutron does not have an electrical charge.

Around the nucleus are sub-atomic particles called electrons. Each electron has a negative electrical charge and travels at about the speed of light as it moves around the nucleus.

The number of electrons around the nucleus is the same as the number of protons in the nucleus. The negative electrical charges on the electrons are balanced by the positive electrical charges on the protons. This balancing of the charges makes the atom electrically neutral – it has no electrical charge.

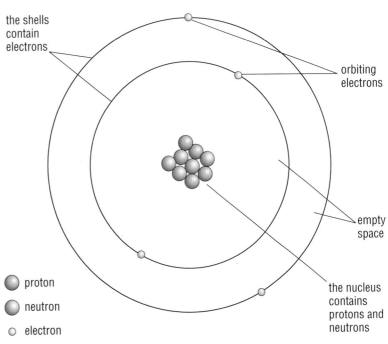

the shells contain electrons

orbiting electrons

empty space

the nucleus contains protons and neutrons

○ proton
○ neutron
○ electron

**Figure 4.2** The basic structure of the atom, e.g. a beryllium atom.

**5** 'The nucleus and the electrons in an atom are like the Sun and the planets in the Solar System.' How good is this statement at explaining the structure of the atom?

**6** How many electrons are there in each shell of an atom of lead?

The electrons are arranged in groups at different distances from the nucleus. They are described as being arranged in shells. For example, the carbon atom has two electrons close to the nucleus making an inner shell and four electrons further away making an outer shell. Many atoms have more shells than this. For example, the lead atom has six shells.

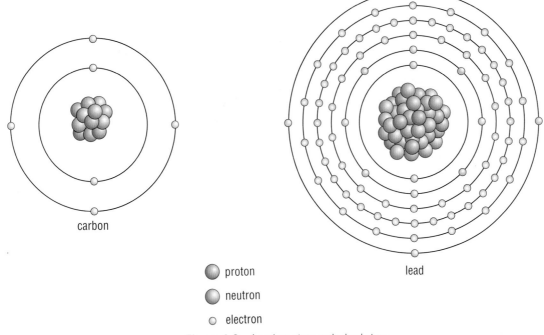

carbon

lead

○ proton
○ neutron
○ electron

**Figure 4.3** A carbon atom and a lead atom.

**7** What are isotopes?

All the atoms in each element have the same number of protons. For example, carbon atoms always have six protons and sodium atoms always have eleven protons.

The number of neutrons in the atoms of an element may vary. Most carbon atoms, for example, have six neutrons but about 1% of carbon atoms have seven neutrons and an even smaller amount of carbon atoms have eight neutrons. These atoms of an element that have different numbers of neutrons are called isotopes.

## The fourth state of matter

Inside stars the temperature is so high that the atoms break up. Some of the electrons break away from the rest of the particles in the atom. The remaining particles form an electrically charged structure called an ion. This mixture of electrons and ions in a star is called a plasma.

Plasma can also be made on the Earth by using low pressures in a glass container. If the container has an electrically charged rod at its centre the plasma will carry electricity to the glass. The path of electricity is shown by a flash of light through the plasma.

**1** How is plasma different from other states of matter?

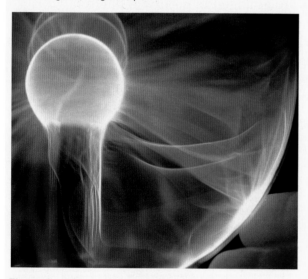

**Figure A**  Plasma carrying electricity in a glass container.

## Chemical symbols

Alchemists investigated materials in an attempt to find a way to make gold or a medicine which would extend the human life span. They wrote down details of their investigations using symbols to represent the substances they used or produced. The use of symbols saved them time. Figure 4.4 shows a few of the symbols used by alchemists.

## Explanation of the Chimical Characters — p.99.

| Term | Term | Term | Term |
|---|---|---|---|
| Steele iron or Mars | celestial signe | Gumme | Crocus |
| Loadstone | Cancer | Hower | martis |
| Ayre | another ... 69 | Oyle | Sagitari a celestial sign |
| Lymbeck | Ashes | Day | Soap |
| Allom | Pot Ashes | Gemini a celestial signe | Scorpi a Celestial sign |
| Amalgama aaa | Calx ... C | Leo another signe | Salt alkali |
| Antimony | Quick lime | Stratū sug stratū or lay upon lay ... SSS | Armoniac Salt |
| Aquarius a signe of the zodiack | Cinnabar or Vermillion | Marcassite | Comōn Salt |
| Silver or Luna | Waxe | Precipitate of Quicksilv | Salgemme |
| Quicksilver or Mercury | Crucible | Sublimate | Brimstō or sulph |
| Aries another | Calcinated copper æs ustū or crocus veneris | Moneth | Black sulphur |
| Celestial signe | Note of Distillation | Niter or Saltpeter | Philosophers sulphur |
| Arsenich | Water | Night | To sublimate |
| Balneum ... B | Aqua fortis | Gold or Sol | Talck ... X |
| Balneum | aqua Regalis | Auripigmentū | Tartar |
| Maris ... MB | Spirit | Lead or Saturne | Taur a Celestial signe |
| Vaporous | SP. | Pisces a Celestial signe | Earth |
| Bath ... VB | Spirit of Wyn | Powder | Caput Mortuū |
| Libra another celestial signe | Tinne or Jupiter | To precipitate | Tuty |
| Borax | Powder of Bricks | To purify | Glasse |
| Bricks | Fire | Quintessency ... QE | Vert degrice, or flower of Copper |
| Capricornus another | | Realgar | Vinegar |
| | | Retorte | Distilled Vinegar |
| | | Sand | Vitriol |
| | | | Urine |

**Figure 4.4** Alchemists' symbols.

Many of the substances had been given a number of different names by different alchemists. When chemists began their work they used the alchemists' names, but this soon led to confusion.

With the development of Boyle's idea of the elements, it was decided that each substance used in an investigation or produced from it should be clearly identified by one name only so that reports of investigations could be clearly understood.

In 1787 Lavoisier and three other scientists set out the names of all the substances used in chemical investigations in a three hundred page book.

In 1813 Jöns Jakob Berzelius introduced the symbols we still use to represent the elements. Each element was identified by the first letter of its name. If two or more elements began with the same letter another letter in the name was also used.

**8** Why do some elements have two letters for their chemical symbol and others have only one?

**9** Why isn't the symbol for silver S, and the symbol for potassium P?

**10** How did some elements get their names?

Some of the symbols are made from old names for the elements. Iron, for example, had an old name of ferrum and the symbol Fe is made from it. Silver was known as argentum and its symbol is Ag.

Sodium is known as natrium, and potassium is known as kalium in Latin and some other languages, and their symbols have been made from these names. The symbol for sodium is Na and the symbol for potassium is K.

The elements have received their names from a variety of sources. Some elements such as chlorine (from the Greek word meaning green colour) and bromine (from the Greek word for stench) are named after their properties. Other elements are named after places. The places may be as small as a village – strontium is named after Strontian in Scotland – or as large as a planet – uranium is named after the planet Uranus. A few elements, such as einsteinium, are named after people.

## ◆ SUMMARY ◆

◆ Substances can be broken down into elements *(see page 47)*.
◆ Each element is composed of atoms *(see page 52)*.
◆ An atom contains protons, neutrons and electrons *(see page 52)*.
◆ There is a chemical symbol for each element *(see page 54)*.

### *End of chapter question*

**1** The particle theory describes materials as being made up from tiny spheres like microscopic table tennis balls. How good is this model in explaining the structure of the atom? Explain your answer.

# 5 Chemical reactions

The changes of state described in Chapter 2 are relatively easy to bring about. When substances take part in a chemical reaction, one or more new substances are created. It is sometimes easy to reverse these chemical changes and make the original substances but often it is not possible. A chemical reaction occurs when a chemical compound is broken down into new substances or when substances are joined together to make new chemical compounds.

## Reactants and products

The substances that take part in the reaction are called the reactants. The substances that form as a result of the chemical reaction are called the products:

reactants → products

Chemists use chemical equations to describe the chemical reactions. They save time and space and provide the essential information about the reaction in an easy-to-read form. The simplest chemical equations are word equations. More complicated equations which give more detail of how the chemicals are combined are given in formula equations (see Chapter 14).

In an equation the reactants are written on the left hand side and the products on the right hand side. If two or more reactants or products are featured in the equation they are linked together by plus (+) signs:

reactant A + reactant B → product C + product D

An arrow points from the reactants to the products. Most reactions are not reversible and there is only one arrow. Some reactions are reversible (they can go in either direction) and a special arrow sign points in both directions:

$$A + B \rightleftharpoons C + D$$

## Chemical reactions and energy

When a chemical reaction takes place energy may be given out or taken in.

Examples of reactions that give out energy are the burning of gas in a Bunsen burner and the explosion of petrol vapour in a car engine.

1 What is the difference between a product and a reactant in a chemical reaction?
2 How can you tell from the equation if the reaction is reversible or not?

An example of a reaction that takes in energy is photosynthesis. This takes place in the leaves and other green parts of plants. Light energy is taken in from sunlight and is used as carbon dioxide and water combine to form sugar. The decomposition of limestone to make lime (see page 60) is another reaction that takes in energy. Heat is required to start and maintain the reaction.

**Figure 5.1**  Photosynthesis is a reaction that takes in energy from sunlight.

**3** What changes in energy can occur when chemical reactions take place?

**4** Why is it that you must put a match flame to a candle wick to light it but can remove the match when the wick starts to burn?

Some chemical reactions need a little energy to make them start and then they can continue on their own. The energy required to start the reaction is usually provided in the form of heat. The reaction taking place on a burning match head provides the energy to make the wax burn on a candle wick.

# Types of chemical reaction
## Decomposition

One of the simplest types of reaction is called decomposition. There is only one reactant and it breaks down into two or more products.

### *Thermal decomposition*

The most common type of decomposition is called thermal decomposition. In this case a compound is heated and it breaks down into other substances – the products. For example, the wax in a burning candle on a birthday cake breaks down to carbon dioxide and water vapour.

**Figure 5.2**   A burning candle is an example of thermal decomposition.

### Heating limestone

A simple thermal decomposition can be performed by heating a small piece of limestone. Limestone is made of a compound called calcium carbonate. The heat breaks down the compound into calcium oxide and carbon dioxide. The word equation for this reaction is:

calcium carbonate → calcium oxide + carbon dioxide

Calcium oxide does not break down when it is heated, but at very high temperatures it becomes incandescent and gives out a bright white light known as limelight. This was used to light the stages of theatres before electricity was available and gave rise to the expression 'in the limelight'.

**Figure 5.3**   The 'limelight man' in an old theatre.

### Limestone – a useful raw material

Limestone and the products of its thermal decomposition have several uses. Limestone is used in the extraction of iron from its ore (see page 126), it is mixed with sand and sodium carbonate to make glass and is ground up, mixed with clay and then heated to make cement.

Calcium oxide has two common names: lime and quicklime. Large amounts of limestone are converted into lime in a lime kiln (see Figure 5.4). Small limestone rocks are poured into the top of a kiln, which is then sealed. Heat from gas burners decomposes the limestone. Streams of air entering the bottom of the kiln carry away carbon dioxide from the top of the kiln and prevent it reacting with the calcium oxide. If the carbon dioxide did react with the calcium oxide, calcium carbonate would form again.

Lime is used to neutralise the acidic conditions in soils which reduce crop production. Figure 6.10 shows how it is spread on the soil.

When lime comes into contact with water it expands as it absorbs the water and some steam is produced. The product of the reaction is calcium hydroxide. The common name for calcium hydroxide is slaked lime. This is used in the building industry with sand and water to make mortar for holding bricks together.

Lime water is a dilute solution of calcium hydroxide. It is used to test for carbon dioxide gas. If a gas is thought to be carbon dioxide, it is bubbled through lime water. If carbon dioxide is present, a chemical reaction takes place in which calcium carbonate is made. This white substance is insoluble in water and forms a white precipitate which makes the lime water cloudy or milky.

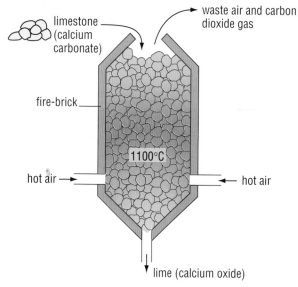

**Figure 5.4** A lime kiln.

5 If air was not allowed to stream through the kiln, how would the production of lime be affected? Explain your answer.

6 The heating of calcium carbonate can be considered a reversible reaction (see page 57).
  a) Explain why this is so.
  b) Construct an equation to show that the reaction is reversible.

7 Write a word equation for the production of slaked lime.

Clear lime water

Carbon dioxide is bubbled through

Lime water turns cloudy

**Figure 5.5** A test for carbon dioxide.

### Heating copper carbonate

Copper carbonate is a green powder. If it is heated strongly it breaks down into black copper oxide and carbon dioxide.

The equation for this reaction is:

copper carbonate → copper oxide + carbon dioxide

**Figure 5.6**   Before (left) and after (right) the heating of copper carbonate.

### Heating copper sulphate crystals

Copper sulphate crystals are blue but when they are heated they decompose to a white powder and water vapour. The water vapour can be condensed to form liquid water.

If the liquid water is added to the white powder, blue copper sulphate is produced again. The blue copper sulphate is called hydrated copper sulphate and the white copper sulphate is called anhydrous copper sulphate.

The equation for this reversible reaction is:

hydrated copper sulphate ⇌ anhydrous copper sulphate + water

**8** What happens in a decomposition reaction?

**Figure 5.7**   Before (left) and after (right) the heating of copper sulphate.

**9** Cobalt chloride exists both as a pink hydrated form and a blue anhydrous form. The hydrated form can be decomposed in a similar way to copper sulphate. Construct a word equation for the reaction.

### Test for water vapour

Anhydrous copper sulphate is used to test for the presence of water vapour in the air. If water vapour is present the copper sulphate changes colour from white to blue as hydrated copper sulphate is formed.

Cobalt chloride is also used to test for water vapour as it too has hydrated and anhydrous forms. The anhydrous form is blue. It turns pink in the presence of water.

### Heating potassium permanganate

Potassium permanganate is a purple crystalline solid which is a compound of potassium, manganese and oxygen. When it is heated it breaks down and releases oxygen. The gas can be collected as shown in Figure 5.8.

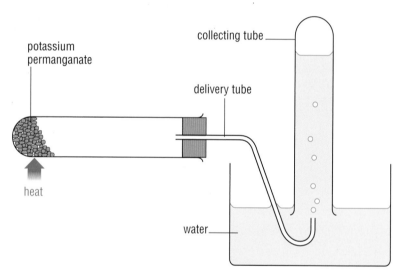

**Figure 5.8** The heating of potassium permanganate.

### Heating some metal oxides

Not all compounds break down when they are heated. For example, when copper oxide, magnesium oxide and zinc oxides are heated each metal remains combined with oxygen.

## *Decomposition by light*

When light shines on silver chloride it decomposes into tiny black crystals of silver metal and chlorine gas. The equation for this reaction is:

$$\text{silver chloride} \rightarrow \text{silver} + \text{chlorine}$$

Also see page 174 for the use of this kind of reaction in photography. Some compounds used in dyes to colour fabrics in clothes and curtains are changed by the action of light.

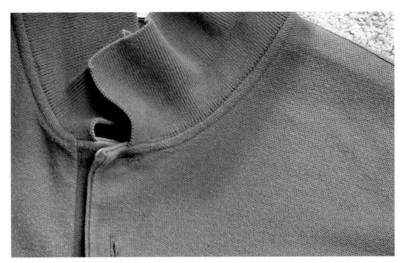

**Figure 5.9**   The dye under the collar, which is usually covered, has not been affected by sunlight.

## *Decomposition by electricity*

Electricity can be used to decompose substances which have been melted and are in liquid form, or are in solution. Water (molten ice) can be decomposed into hydrogen and oxygen. The equation for this reaction is:

$$\text{water} \rightarrow \text{hydrogen} + \text{oxygen}$$

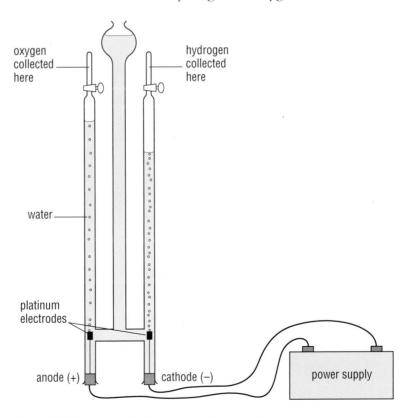

**Figure 5.10**   Apparatus for the decomposition of water.

## Synthesis

When two or more substances take part in a chemical reaction to make one compound the reaction is called a synthesis.

### Iron sulphide

When iron and sulphur are heated together in a fume cupboard they form iron sulphide:

iron + sulphur → iron sulphide

### Magnesium oxide

When magnesium is heated in air, the oxygen in the air combines with the magnesium to form magnesium oxide:

magnesium + oxygen → magnesium oxide

During this reaction large amounts of heat and light are released. This synthesis reaction is a major feature of all firework displays.

**Figure 5.11** A firework display.

10 How is a synthesis reaction different from a decomposition reaction?

## Oxidation and reduction

These two kinds of reaction may take place separately or together.

### Oxidation

An oxidation reaction takes place when oxygen is added to a substance, or hydrogen is removed from it. The reaction between magnesium and oxygen is an oxidation reaction; magnesium is oxidised.

When the gas, methane, burns in a Bunsen burner, an oxidation reaction takes place. Methane is made of carbon and hydrogen. In this reaction both elements combine with oxygen. Water is a compound of hydrogen and oxygen.

methane + oxygen → carbon dioxide + water

## *Reduction*

A reduction takes place when oxygen is taken from a substance, or hydrogen is added to it.

When copper oxide powder is heated in a stream of hydrogen gas, the hydrogen combines with the oxygen in the copper oxide to form water and the copper is left behind. The copper is reduced.

copper oxide + hydrogen → copper + water vapour

In this reaction an oxidation has also taken place. The hydrogen has been oxidised because it has combined with oxygen to form water.

**11** What is the difference between an oxidation reaction and a reduction reaction?

**12** Why is it possible for both these reactions to take place at once?

## Neutralisation

Acids and bases are described in Chapter 6. They have properties which are 'opposite' in nature to each other. For example, acids turn a substance called blue litmus from blue to red while bases turn red litmus to blue. Equal quantities of acid and base can be brought together to produce a neutralisation reaction in which the products have properties different from either of the reactants.

The equation for the neutralisation reaction between hydrochloric acid and sodium hydroxide is:

hydrochloric acid + sodium hydroxide → sodium chloride + water

This reaction can be written more generally as:

acid + base → salt + water

See page 70 for more information on salts.

## Displacement

In this reaction one substance replaces another substance in a compound. For example, acids contain hydrogen and when an acid is brought into contact with a metal, the metal displaces the hydrogen. Hydrochloric acid is made up of hydrogen and chlorine.

iron + hydrochloric acid → iron chloride + hydrogen

The iron forms iron chloride which dissolves in the water in the acidic solution. The hydrogen forms bubbles which escape from the surface of the liquid with a fizzing sound.

## Precipitation

Some solutions can be mixed together to produce a precipitate. This is formed by tiny particles that do not dissolve in the mixture of the solutions. The precipitate makes the liquid cloudy.

If silver nitrate solution is poured into a solution of sodium chloride, a chemical reaction takes place which produces silver chloride. This forms a white precipitate.

$$\text{silver nitrate} + \text{sodium chloride} \rightarrow \text{silver chloride} + \text{sodium nitrate}$$

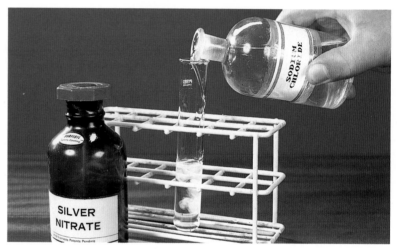

**Figure 5.12**   The precipitation of silver chloride.

## Fermentation

This chemical reaction takes place through the action of a living organism – yeast. Yeast is mixed with a sugar solution and enclosed in an airtight chamber. In these conditions the yeast cannot respire aerobically, using oxygen from the air to release energy from the sugar and produce carbon dioxide and water. Instead, the yeast respires anaerobically, a process in which some of the sugar is converted into ethanol. This reaction allows the yeast to be used to make alcoholic drinks. The carbon dioxide produced in fermentation is also used to make bread rise before it is baked. The ethanol produced in the reaction evaporates when the bread is baked.

**Figure 5.13**   The spaces are caused by carbon dioxide gas being trapped during baking.

$$\text{sugar} \rightarrow \text{ethanol} + \text{carbon dioxide}$$

# Speed of chemical reactions

The speed of a chemical reaction depends on the temperature of the reactants, their concentration and the area of contact between them. It can also be changed by the use of a catalyst.

## Temperature and reaction speed

The speed of the reaction increases if the temperature is raised and decreases if the temperature is lowered. If the temperature of the reactants is raised by 10°C the speed of the reaction may be doubled.

## Concentration and reaction speed

If the concentration of one of the reactants is increased the speed of the reaction increases. If the concentration is reduced the speed of the reaction decreases. If the concentration of one of the reactants is doubled the speed of the reaction may be doubled.

## Surface area and reaction speed

The size of the surface area of a solid in contact with a liquid affects the speed of the reaction between them. If a large piece of solid is broken up into smaller pieces the surface area of the solid in contact with the liquid increases, and the speed of the reaction between them increases.

## Catalyst

A catalyst is a substance which is added to the reactants to change the speed of the reaction between them. It is not changed in the reaction. In industrial processes such as the manufacture of sulphuric acid (see page 141) catalysts are used to speed up reactions. In the manufacture of many packaged food products such as crisps, catalysts called antioxidants are added to prevent substances in the food reacting with oxygen in the air and making the food go bad.

Chemical reactions take place in living things and there are catalysts present in the body to control them. The catalysts are called enzymes. There is a different enzyme for each chemical reaction. Enzymes are made of proteins, which are destroyed by strong heat. Catalysts made from other substances such as metals are not destroyed in this way.

13 Two cartons of milk were opened and one was left by a radiator while the other was placed in a fridge. How will the milk in the two cartons differ after 3 days? Explain your answer.

14 In a model volcano some vinegar was poured onto sodium bicarbonate. A reaction took place which produced a fizzy liquid which flowed down the sides of the volcano like lava. If water is added to the vinegar and the reaction is repeated, will the eruption of the volcano be stronger or weaker? Explain your answer.

15 a) What is the surface area of a cube with sides that are 2 cm long?
   b) The cube is cut into eight cubes each with a side 1 cm long. What is the surface area of these eight cubes?
   c) How does the surface area of the eight cubes compare with the surface area of the one large cube?

16 Two blood-stained cloths were placed in separate bowls of water. A biological washing powder containing enzymes was added to one bowl, while nothing else was added to the second bowl. After a while, the two cloths were removed from the bowls and examined. How do you think they would compare? Explain your answer.

# ◆ SUMMARY ◆

♦ Chemical reactions occur when substances are broken down or joined together to make new substances *(see page 57)*.

♦ A chemical equation features reactants and products separated by an arrow *(see page 57)*.

♦ Chemical reactions may give out or take in heat energy *(see page 57)*.

♦ Chemicals can be decomposed (broken down) by heat *(see page 58)*.

♦ Some substances can be decomposed by light *(see page 62)*.

♦ Water and many other substances can be decomposed by electricity *(see page 63)*.

♦ A synthesis reaction takes place when two or more substances combine and make a chemical compound *(see page 64)*.

♦ An oxidation reaction takes place when oxygen is added to a substance or hydrogen is taken away from it *(see page 64)*.

♦ A reduction reaction takes place when oxygen is taken from a substance or hydrogen is added to it *(see page 65)*.

♦ A neutralisation reaction occurs when equal quantities of acid and base are brought together *(see page 65)*.

♦ In a displacement reaction, one substance replaces another substance in a compound *(see page 65)*.

♦ A precipitation reaction takes place when some solutions are mixed together and produce a new compound that does not dissolve *(see page 66)*.

♦ A fermentation reaction takes place through the action of a living organism such as yeast and in the absence of oxygen *(see page 66)*.

♦ The speed of the reaction depends on the temperature, concentration and surface area of the reactants as well as on the use of catalysts *(see page 67)*.

## *End of chapter questions*

**1** Complete this word equation and state what kind of reaction it describes:

sulphuric acid + sodium hydroxide →

**2** Is fermentation like a decomposition reaction? Explain your answer.

# 6 Acids and bases

## Acids

Most people think of acids as corrosive liquids which fizz when they come into contact with solids and burn when they touch the skin. This description is true for many acids and when they are being transported the container holding them has the hazard symbol shown in Figure 6.1.

corrosive **Figure 6.1** The hazard symbol for a corrosive substance.

Some acids are not corrosive and are found in our food. They give some foods their sour taste. This property gave acids their name. The word acid comes from the Latin word *acidus* meaning sour.

Many acids are found in living things. Tables 6.1 and 6.2 show some acids found in plants and animals.

**Table 6.1** Acids found in plants.

| Acid | Plant origin |
|------|------|
| citric acid | orange and lemon juice |
| tartaric acid | grapes |
| ascorbic acid | vitamin C in citrus fruits and blackcurrants |
| methanoic acid | nettle sting |

**Table 6.2** Acids found in animals.

| Acid | Animal origin |
|------|------|
| hydrochloric acid | human stomach |
| lactic acid | muscles during vigorous exercise |
| uric acid | urine, excretory product from DNA in food |
| methanoic acid | ant sting |

**Figure 6.2** Animals and plants that produce acid.

## The acid in vinegar

Ethanoic acid is found in vinegar and is produced as wine becomes sour. The wine contains ethanol, produced by fermentation (see page 66) and also has some oxygen dissolved in it from the air. Over a period of time, the oxygen reacts with the ethanol and converts it to ethanoic acid. This is an oxidation reaction (see page 64) and the reaction happens more quickly if the wine bottle is left uncorked.

**1** Why does wine go sour faster if the cork is removed from the bottle?

## Organic acids and mineral acids

The acids produced by plants and animals (with the exception of hydrochloric acid) are known as organic acids. Ethanoic acid is an organic acid and was the first to be used in experiments. Over the period AD750–1600 the mineral acids were discovered by alchemists. The first mineral acid to be discovered was nitric acid. It was used to separate silver and gold. When the acid was applied to a mixture of the two metals it dissolved the silver but not the gold. Later, sulphuric acid and then hydrochloric acid were discovered. These mineral acids are much stronger (see page 73) than ethanoic acid and allow more chemical reactions to be made. The use of these acids led to many chemical discoveries.

**2** How do you think the terms
  **a)** organic acids and
  **b)** mineral acids came to be used?

**3** Acids in the laboratory are stored in labelled bottles as shown in Figure 6.3.

**Figure 6.3** Bottles of dilute and concentrated acids.

**a)** Which acids are dilute and which are concentrated?
**b)** How is a dilute solution different from a concentrated one?

## Acids and metals

Some metals react with acids and produce a salt and hydrogen. The term salt is used in everyday language for the compound sodium chloride. In chemistry it can mean any metal compound made from an acid. The general word equation for the reaction between a metal and an acid is:

metal + acid → salt + hydrogen

An example of this is the reaction between zinc and hydrochloric acid. The word equation for this reaction is:

zinc + hydrochloric acid → zinc chloride + hydrogen

Figure 6.4 shows the apparatus and reactants set up to demonstrate this reaction.

**4** Bubbles of hydrogen are released from the surface of the acid and build up a high gas pressure in the flask. What do you think happens next to
**a)** the hydrogen in the flask,
**b)** the water in the test-tube?
**5** Write a word equation for the reaction between magnesium and sulphuric acid.

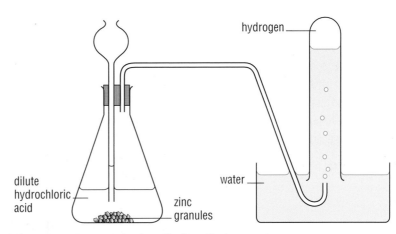

**Figure 6.4** Apparatus for the collection of hydrogen.

## Acids and carbonates

A carbonate is a compound that contains carbon and oxygen combined together. When a carbonate reacts with an acid, carbon dioxide is released and a salt and water form. This reaction may be written as a general word equation as:

carbonate + acid → carbon dioxide + salt + water

An example of this is the reaction between magnesium carbonate and hydrochloric acid. The word equation for this reaction is:

**6** Write the word equation for the reaction between sulphuric acid and copper carbonate.

$$\text{magnesium carbonate} + \text{hydrochloric acid} \rightarrow \text{magnesium chloride} + \text{water} + \text{carbon dioxide}$$

## Bases

The neutralisation reaction described on page 65 shows that bases react with acids to form salts and water. In this reaction the properties of the acid and the base are cancelled out and products with neutral properties – the salt and the water – are produced. As bases neutralise acids they are sometimes described as having properties which are opposite to acids. The compounds that are bases are metal oxides, hydroxides, carbonates or hydrogencarbonates.

Some bases are soluble in water. They are called alkalis. Sodium hydroxide and potassium hydroxide are examples of alkalis that are used in laboratories. A concentrated solution of an alkali is corrosive and can burn the skin. The same hazard symbol as the one used for acids (see Figure 6.1) is used on containers of alkalis when they are transported.

**7** Which of the following compounds are bases – copper chloride, sodium hydroxide, calcium carbonate, magnesium sulphate, copper oxide, lead nitrate, sodium hydrogencarbonate?

Even dilute solutions of alkali such as dilute sodium hydroxide solution react with fat on the surface of the skin and change it into substances found in soap. Many household cleaners used for cleaning metal, floors and ovens contain alkalis and must be handled with great care.

**Figure 6.5**  Alkalis used in the home.

# Detecting acids and alkalis

Some substances change colour when an acid or an alkali is added to them. Litmus is a substance which is extracted from a living organism called lichen. In chemistry it is used as a solution or is absorbed onto paper strips. Litmus solution is purple but it turns red when it comes into contact with an acid. Litmus paper for testing for acids is blue. The paper turns red when it is dipped in acid or a drop of acid is put on it. When an alkali comes into contact with purple litmus solution the solution turns blue. Litmus paper used for testing for an alkali is red. When red litmus paper comes into contact with an alkali it turns blue.

Hydrangeas have pink flowers when they are grown in a soil containing lime and blue flowers when grown in a lime-free soil. The colour of the flowers can be used to assess the alkalinity of the soil.

**Figure 6.6**  Pink and blue hydrangeas.

**8** Why are bases sometimes described as the opposite of acids?

**9** How are acids and bases similar?

Universal indicator (see below) turns purple, blue, yellow, beige, pink or red when it comes into contact with an acid or alkali. The colour shows how weak or strong the acid is.

# Strong and weak acids and alkalis

The strength of an acid or alkali does not describe whether the solution is dilute or concentrated. It describes the ability of a substance to form particles called ions. Acids form hydrogen ions and alkalis form hydroxide ions. A strong acid forms a large number of hydrogen ions in solution and a weak acid forms a small number of hydrogen ions in solution. A strong alkali forms a large number of hydroxide ions in solution and a weak alkali forms a small number of hydroxide ions in solution. The strength of an acid or alkali is measured on the pH scale. On this scale the strongest acid is 0 and the strongest alkali is 14. A solution with a pH of 7 is neutral. It is neither an acid nor an alkali. A strong acid has a pH of 0–2, a weak acid has a pH of 3–6, a weak alkali has a pH of 8–11 and a strong alkali has a pH of 12–14.

An electrical instrument called a pH meter is used to measure the pH of an acid or alkali accurately.

**10** Here are some measurements of solutions that were made using a pH meter: **A** 0, **B** 11, **C** 6, **D** 3, **E** 13, **F** 8.
   **a)** Which of the solutions are
      **i)** acids, **ii)** alkalis?
   **b)** If the solutions were tested with universal indicator paper, what colour would the indicator paper be with each one?
   **c)** Fresh milk has a pH of 6. How do you think the pH would change as it became sour? Explain your answer.

**Figure 6.7** A pH meter in use.

For general laboratory use, the pH of an acid or an alkali is measured with universal indicator. This is made from a mixture of indicators. Each indicator changes colour over part of the range of the scale. By combining the indicators together, a solution is made that gives various colours over the whole of the pH range (see Figure 6.8).

11 Here are some results of solutions tested with universal indicator paper:
sulphuric acid – red,
metal polish – dark blue,
washing-up liquid – yellow,
milk of magnesia – light blue,
oven cleaner – purple,
car battery acid – pink.
Arrange the solutions in order of their pH, starting with the one with the lowest pH.

12 Identify the strong and weak acids and alkalis from the results shown in questions 10 and 11.

13 Look at page 70 about acids and predict whether nitric acid is a strong or a weak acid. Explain your answer.

14 A sample of acid rain turned universal indicator yellow. What would you expect its pH to be? Is it a strong or a weak acid?

15 Write word equations for the reactions between
a) sulphuric acid and zinc oxide,
b) hydrochloric acid and calcium hydroxide,
c) nitric acid and calcium carbonate.

16 How is the neutralisation of a carbonate different from the neutralisation of an oxide or a hydroxide?

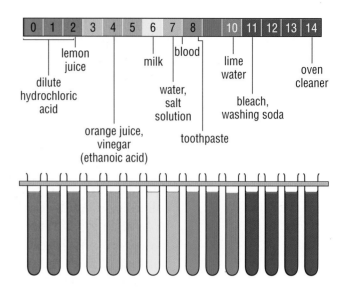

**Figure 6.8** The pH scale and universal indicator.

# Neutralisation

When an acid reacts with a base a process called neutralisation occurs in which a salt and water are formed. This reaction can be written as a general word equation:

$$\text{acid} + \text{base} \rightarrow \text{salt} + \text{water}$$

Specific examples of neutralisation reactions are:

sulphuric acid + magnesium oxide → magnesium sulphate + water

hydrochloric acid + sodium hydroxide → sodium chloride + water

hydrochloric acid + zinc carbonate → zinc chloride + water + carbon dioxide

nitric acid + sodium hydrogencarbonate → sodium nitrate + water + carbon dioxide

## Using neutralisation reactions

When you are stung by a nettle, the burning sensation on your skin is caused by methanoic acid. You can neutralise the acid by rubbing a dock leaf on the wound. As you press the dock leaf against the wound, a base in the leaf juices reacts with the acid in the sting and neutralises it so the burning sensation stops.

A bee sting is acidic and may be neutralised by soap, which is an alkali. A wasp sting is alkaline and may be neutralised with vinegar which is a weak acid. Sometimes the stomach produces too much acid, which causes indigestion. The acid is neutralised by taking a tablet containing either magnesium hydroxide, calcium carbonate, aluminium hydroxide or sodium hydrogencarbonate (see Figure 6.9).

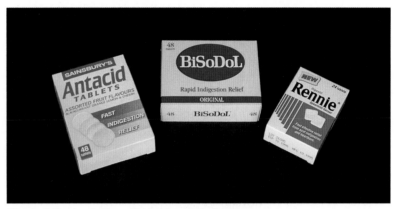

**Figure 6.9** A selection of tablets to cure indigestion.

Lime is used to neutralise acidity in soil. When it is applied to fields it makes them appear temporarily white, as Figure 6.10 shows.

**Figure 6.10** Liming fields to improve crop production.

The soda–acid fire extinguisher contains a bottle of sulphuric acid and a solution of sodium hydrogencarbonate (see Figure 6.11). When the plunger is struck or the extinguisher is turned upside down, the acid mixes with the sodium hydrogencarbonate solution and a neutralisation reaction takes place. The pressure of the carbon dioxide produced in the reaction pushes the water out of the extinguisher and onto the fire.

**Figure 6.11**  A soda–acid fire extinguisher.

## ◆ SUMMARY ◆

◆ Some acids are made by living things *(see page 69)*.
◆ Ethanoic acid in vinegar is made by the oxidation of ethanol in wine *(see page 70)*.
◆ The mineral acids are nitric acid, sulphuric acid and hydrochloric acid *(see page 70)*.
◆ An acid reacts with a metal to produce a salt and hydrogen *(see page 70)*.
◆ An acid reacts with a carbonate to produce a salt, water and carbon dioxide *(see page 71)*.
◆ Bases are metal oxides, hydroxides, carbonates and hydrogencarbonates *(see page 71)*.
◆ Bases that dissolve in water are called alkalis *(see page 71)*.
◆ An acid can be detected by its ability to turn blue litmus paper red *(see page 72)*.
◆ An alkali can be detected by its ability to turn red litmus paper blue *(see page 72)*.
◆ The strength of an acid or an alkali depends on the number of ions it contains *(see page 73)*.
◆ The pH scale is used to measure the degree of acidity or alkalinity of a liquid *(see page 73)*.
◆ When an acid reacts with a base a neutralisation reaction takes place *(see page 74)*.
◆ Neutralisation reactions have a wide range of uses *(see page 74)*.

## *End of chapter questions*

**1**  Write an account entitled 'The acids in our lives'.
**2**  How can you tell when an acid has neutralised an alkali?

# 7 Air

The air that we breathe is part of the atmosphere which is a mixture of gases that covers the surface of the Earth. It stretches out into space for about 1000 km.

It is believed that the atmosphere was produced by a process known as out-gassing. In this process, gases from inside the Earth are released through volcanoes (see page 93). It began when the Earth formed and continues to the present day.

The atmosphere is divided into five layers (see Figure 7.1). The composition of the gases in the atmosphere changes as you pass through the layers from outer space to the Earth's surface.

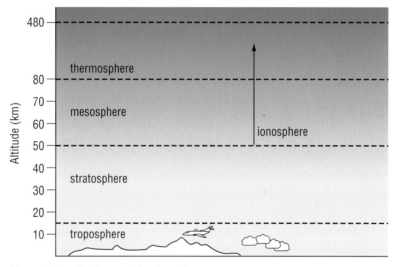

**Figure 7.1** The layers of the atmosphere.

In the exosphere the mixture of gases is 25% helium and 75% hydrogen. As you sink through the thermosphere and mesosphere, the amount of hydrogen in the atmosphere falls to zero, the amount of helium falls to 15% and the amounts of nitrogen and oxygen rise to 70% and 15% respectively.

In the stratosphere the composition of gases is 1% ozone, 1% argon, 18% oxygen and 80% nitrogen. The composition of the air in the troposphere is shown in Figure 7.2.

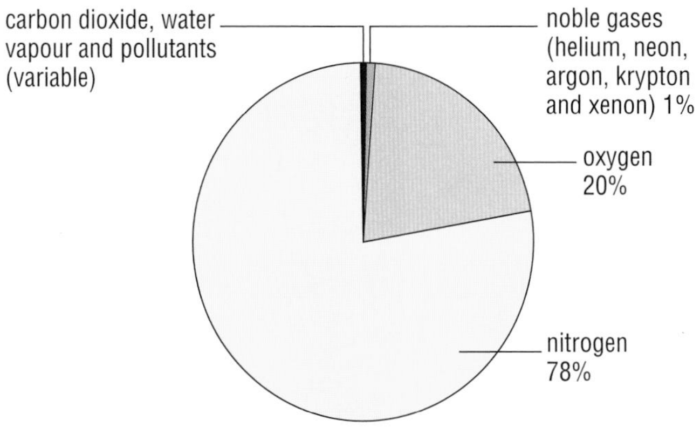

carbon dioxide, water vapour and pollutants (variable)

noble gases (helium, neon, argon, krypton and xenon) 1%

oxygen 20%

nitrogen 78%

**Figure 7.2** The composition of the air near the Earth's surface.

# Liquid air and the discovery of some noble gases

Karl von Linde (1842–1934), a German chemist, devised a way of making air so cold that it turned into a liquid. Figure A shows in very simple form the apparatus he used to turn air into a liquid.

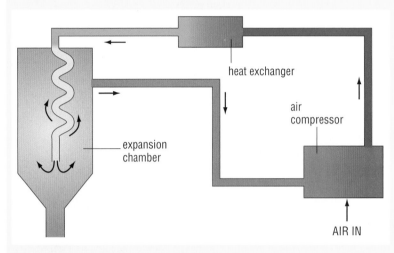

heat exchanger

air compressor

expansion chamber

AIR IN

**Figure A**   Von Linde's apparatus to liquefy air.

1  How can dust be removed from air?
2  The freezing point of water is 0°C and carbon dioxide becomes a solid at −78°C. How do you think water vapour and carbon dioxide are removed from the air?
3  By how much does the air pressure drop in the expansion chamber?
4  Why does oxygen not turn into a gas at the top of the fractionating column?
5  Who was Ramsay's assistant in the discovery of three noble gases (see Table 4.1 page 50)?

Before the air is allowed to enter the compressor, dust, water vapour and carbon dioxide are removed.

Inside the compressor, the air is squashed until its pressure is 200 times atmospheric pressure. As the air is squashed it heats up, so it is moved to a heat exchanger where the heat is removed.

The cold, squashed air then passes into an expansion chamber where its pressure falls to six times atmospheric pressure. As the air expands, it loses more heat and as it moves back to the compressor, it passes over the pipe – bringing in more air. It cools the air in this pipe before it expands. Eventually, as the air circulates through the apparatus some of it cools to −200°C and changes into a liquid. This is moved to a fractionating column (see Figure B) where the gases in the air are separated.

The top of the fractionating column is warm enough for nitrogen (boiling point −196°C) to turn into a gas. It is too cold for oxygen (boiling point −183°C) to turn into a gas so the oxygen remains in liquid form and flows down the column. Argon has a boiling point of −190°C and it is drawn off as a gas from near the middle of the column.

In 1898, William Ramsay (1852–1916) investigated the argon he had collected by fractionating liquid air. He let the liquefied argon boil slowly and discovered that there were more gases mixed with it. The gases were named the Greek neon (meaning new), krypton (meaning hidden) and xenon (meaning stranger).

**Figure B**   A fractionating column at an air separation plant.

# Uses of the air gases

All the gases that make up the air are colourless and do not have a smell, but they have many uses.

## Nitrogen

Nitrogen hardly dissolves in water. It is a neutral gas and is very unreactive with other chemicals, although at the very high temperatures found in a lightning flash it combines with oxygen to form nitrogen dioxide.

As nitrogen is so unreactive it can be used in its gaseous form to replace air in food packaging (see page 90). If nitrogen is cooled to below −196°C it changes into a liquid. In its liquid form nitrogen is used as a coolant because it does not react with the chemicals which make up the parts of a refrigerator. The low temperatures achieved by using liquid nitrogen are used for storing biological tissues such as blood and semen, embryos and organs such as kidneys (see Figure 7.3).

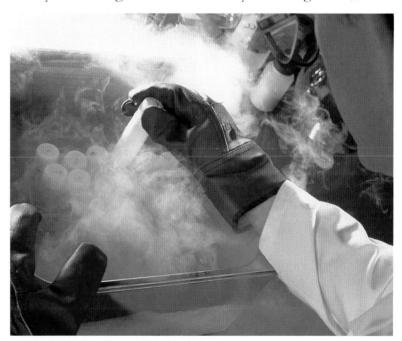

**Figure 7.3**  Storing a sample in liquid nitrogen.

Nitrogen is an essential component of proteins, which are used to form the bodies of plants and animals. It is taken into plants through the roots in the form of minerals called nitrates and passed onto animals when they feed on the plants. Nitrogen is used to make fertiliser to help crop plants grow. Nitrogen is also used to make ammonia and nitric acid which are used in the chemical industry (see Chapter 11).

## Oxygen

Oxygen is a neutral gas. A litre $(1000\,cm^3)$ of air contains $200\,cm^3$ of oxygen. Oxygen dissolves in water, but a litre of water may only hold up to $10\,cm^3$ of oxygen. However, this is enough to support a wide range of different kinds of aquatic life. Oxygen is essential for the process of respiration. In this process, plants and animals release energy which they use to keep themselves alive. In hospitals, additional oxygen is given to patients with respiratory diseases to help them breathe. It is mixed with other gases and stored in cylinders which allow divers to swim underwater and mountaineers to climb at high altitudes where the concentration of oxygen in the air is lower than at sea level.

**Figure 7.4** A sub-aqua diver.

Oxygen reacts with many substances in a process called burning (see page 82). When acetylene is burned in oxygen, temperatures as high as 3200°C can be achieved. This is hot enough to cut through most metals or to weld metals together. Oxygen is also used to burn fuel in rocket engines in space craft.

## Noble gases

The noble gases are very unreactive.

### *Argon*

Argon is used in light bulbs. When electricity passes through the tungsten wire in the filament the metal gets hot. If oxygen were present it would react with the hot tungsten and the filament would quickly become so thin that it would break. Argon is used instead of air containing oxygen because it does not react with the tungsten and the filament lasts longer.

It is also used in making silicon and germanium crystals for the electronics industry.

## Neon

This gas produces a red light when electricity flows through it and is used in lights for advertising displays.

**Figure 7.5** Advertising displays in New York.

## Helium

Helium is lighter than air and is used to lift meteorological balloons into the atmosphere. These balloons carry equipment for collecting information for weather forecasting and relay it by radio to weather stations. Helium is also mixed with oxygen to help deep sea divers breathe underwater.

**Figure 7.6**
Launching a
meteorological balloon.

### *Krypton*

This is used in lamps which produce light of a high intensity, such as those used for airport landing lights and in lighthouses.

### *Xenon*

Xenon is used to make the bright light in a photographer's flash gun.

**1** 'Air is a mixture of useful chemicals.' Is this description correct? Explain your answer.

**Figure 7.7**  Press photograpers, waiting for the film star to appear.

## Combustion

Combustion is an oxidation reaction (see page 64) in which energy is given out as heat. If a flame develops, combustion is then called burning. In burning, energy is also given out as light and sound.

### Burning

**Figure 7.8**  Burning needs to take place in air (or oxygen). The fuel on the left is heating water. The fuel on the right is cooking food on a barbecue.

Many substances are burned to provide heat or light. They are called fuels. Wood, coal, coke, charcoal, oil, diesel oil, petrol, natural gas and wax are examples of fuels. The heat may be used to warm buildings, cook meals, make chemicals in industry, expand gases in vehicle engines and turn water into steam to drive generators in power stations. Some gases and waxes are used to provide light in caravans and tents.

**2** Give a use for each of the fuels listed in the paragraph on burning. How many different uses can you find?

Natural gas is an example of a hydrocarbon. It is made of carbon and hydrogen. When natural gas burns, carbon dioxide and water (hydrogen oxide) are produced. Many other fuels such as coal, coke and petrol contain hydrocarbons (see page 145).

## *Investigating a burning candle*

A candle can be used to investigate how fuels burn.

### Investigation 1

If a burning candle is put under a thistle funnel which is attached to the apparatus shown in Figure 7.9 and the suction pump is switched on, a liquid collects in the U-tube and the lime water turns cloudy.

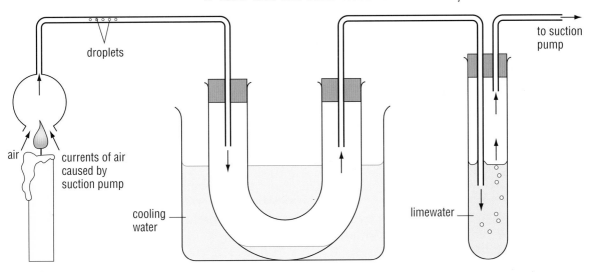

**Figure 7.9**  Testing the products of a burning candle.

When the liquid is tested with cobalt chloride paper, the paper turns from blue to pink. This shows that the liquid is water. The cloudiness in the lime water indicates that carbon dioxide has passed into it.

### Investigation 2

If a beaker is placed over a burning candle, the candle will burn for a while and then go out. A change has taken place in the air that makes it incapable of letting things burn in it.

The test for oxygen is made by plunging a glowing piece of wood into the gas being tested. If the gas is oxygen, the wood bursts into flame. When air from around the burned-out candle is tested for oxygen, the glowing wood goes out. This indicates that oxygen is no longer present. The oxygen in the air under the beaker has been used up by the burning candle.

From the information provided by these two investigations with candles, the following word equation can be set out:

hydrocarbon + oxygen → water + carbon dioxide

Natural gas is a hydrocarbon called methane. When it burns, it breaks down exactly like the hydrocarbons in candle wax. The word equation for this reaction is:

methane + oxygen → carbon dioxide + water

Both of these word equations are examples of complete combustion. This only happens when there is enough oxygen available.

### The danger of incomplete combustion

If there is insufficient oxygen to support complete combustion, incomplete combustion takes place. Carbon monoxide is a very dangerous chemical produced by incomplete combustion. It is produced instead of carbon dioxide. Carbon monoxide is produced in car engines and is released in the exhaust fumes.

Incomplete combustion also occurs when a gas fire has been incorrectly fitted and cannot draw enough oxygen from the room it is heating. Carbon monoxide is a colourless, odourless gas so you do not know when it is being produced. If it is breathed in, it stops the blood taking up oxygen and circulating it round the body. People have died from breathing carbon monoxide from badly fitted fires. All gas fires must be fitted by a trained engineer and used in a well ventilated room so that there is enough air passing through the fire to provide oxygen for complete combustion of the gas.

**3** What happens to the carbon in natural gas when the gas burns in a badly fitted gas fire? Explain your answer.

### The Bunsen burner

The Bunsen burner uses natural gas as a fuel. The parts of a Bunsen burner are shown in Figure 7.10.

The air regulator or collar must be turned to fully close the air hole before the burner is lit. The match should be lit and placed to one side of the top of the chimney before the gas tap is switched on.

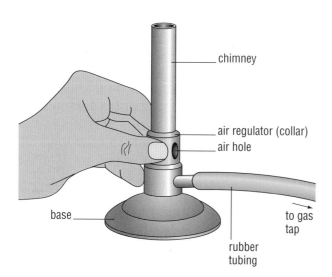

**Figure 7.10** The Bunsen burner.

When the gas is switched on, it shoots out through the jet and up the chimney. Not all the carbon in the gas combines with the oxygen straight away and carbon particles are produced. They are heated to incandescence and give out a yellow light which makes the flame. If this flame is used to heat anything, the carbon particles form soot on the surface of the apparatus being heated.

The flame produced with the air hole closed is called a luminous flame. It is silent. The carbon in the flame reacts with oxygen in the air and forms carbon dioxide.

If the collar is turned and the air hole is fully opened, air mixes with the gas in the chimney. The gases rush up the chimney and form the blue cone of unburnt gas at the top of the chimney. Above the cone, the complete combustion of methane takes place. The flame made when the air hole is completely open is non-luminous and makes a roaring sound.

Less heat energy is released by the luminous flame than the non-luminous flame because the carbon does not all react with oxygen at once. The hottest part of the non-luminous flame is a few millimetres above the tip of the blue cone of unburnt gas.

The size of the flame is controlled by the gas tap on the bench. If the tap is fully open a large flame is produced. A smaller flame is produced by partially closing the gas tap.

## Triangle of fire

The three essentials for a fire are shown in a triangle in Figure 7.11. Remove any side from the triangle of fire and the fire goes out. When fire fighters are trying to put out a fire they may try and remove one or more of the essentials which make up the sides of the triangle. For example, if the fire is near a pile of wood or rubbish that could provide fuel to keep the fire going, the fire fighters will remove it.

**4** Why is one flame hotter than the other?

**5** Why does closing the gas tap a little reduce the size of the flame?

**6** What safety precautions should you take when using a Bunsen burner? Explain the reason for each precaution you take.

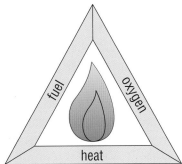

**Figure 7.11**  The fire triangle.

Foam is squirted on a fire to form an airtight 'blanket'. This stops oxygen getting to the fire and helps to put it out. Water is used to reduce the amount of heat and to make the fuel too cool to burn. Water and foam should not be used on electrical appliances that are on fire because they can conduct electricity and could give an electric shock to the fire fighters.

Water must not be used on burning oil or petrol because the water sinks below them. When the water boils, the bubbles break through the oil or petrol and spray it over a wide area. Pouring water on the burning oil in a chip pan would cause burning oil to be sprayed out of the pan – this could set fire to the rest of the kitchen. The fire in the oil can be extinguished by covering the top of the pan with a fire blanket.

**7** After a road accident, petrol and oil that have spilled onto the road are covered with sand. Why?

# Rise and fall of the phlogiston theory

### Development of the theory

Alchemists were concerned with the changes that took place when things burned. Some alchemists weighed the substances before and after burning and discovered that some substances increased in weight after burning. These results were not seen as important as alchemists were more interested in the appearance and properties of the substances they investigated.

Georg Stahl (1660–1734) was a German doctor who developed the phlogiston theory to explain combustion. Stahl believed that phlogiston was something in a combustible substance that allowed it to burn. When the substance burned the phlogiston escaped and the substance that was left behind at the end of the burning process did not possess phlogiston. Air was thought to carry the phlogiston to another substance.

The phlogiston theory was accepted by scientists for over a hundred years, but there were some observations about combustion that it could not easily explain. Scientists thought that when a substance lost phlogiston it would also lose weight, but some of the discoveries of the alchemists showed that the opposite can happen.

### Study of gases

Joannes Baptista van Helmont was a Flemish doctor and alchemist who lived in the late 16th and early 17th Centuries. He noticed that vapours rising into the air from his experiments moved in a chaotic way (see Figure A). He described the matter in these vapours as being in a state of chaos but when he wrote down the word he spelled it as it is spoken in Flemish. He wrote down the word 'gas'. Van Helmont studied burning wood and collected the gas coming from it. He named the gas 'gas sylvestre', which means gas from wood. 'Gas sylvestre' was later found to be carbon dioxide and the word 'gas' became used to describe one of the three states of matter.

**Figure A**

*(continued)*

Up until the 18th Century, chemists only considered the changes in solids and liquids. Although they worked in air contaminated by the gases given off during their experiments they did not consider gases to be important. Stephen Hales (1677–1761) was an English chemist who devised a way to collect gases over water. Figure B shows how gas can be collected over water in the laboratory today.

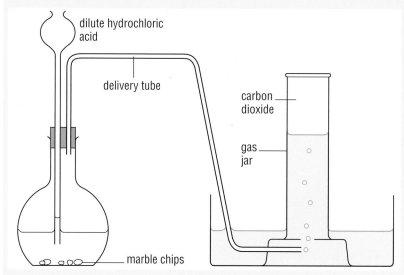

**Figure B**  Collecting a gas over water. The hydrochloric acid reacts with the marble chips to produce carbon dioxide gas. The gas passes from the flask through the delivery tube to the gas jar. As the gas collects in the gas jar it pushes the water out into the trough.

Joseph Black (1728–1799) was a Scottish chemist. He heated limestone so strongly that it gave off a gas which was like 'gas sylvestre' and the solid remaining turned into lime. When he left the lime in air it turned back to a substance like the original limestone. (Although he did not know it, Black had heated calcium carbonate (limestone) and produced carbon dioxide (the gas) and calcium oxide (the lime). When he left the lime in air, carbon dioxide combined with it to make calcium carbonate again.) Black's work showed that the same gas could be produced in different ways – by burning wood and by heating rock. It also showed that gases take part in chemical reactions. Black made many investigations on carbon dioxide. He discovered that substances would not burn in it.

When Joseph Priestley (1733–1804) began studying gases, only three were known. They were air, carbon dioxide and hydrogen. Priestley showed that carbon dioxide was slightly soluble in water. He reasoned that other gases may be soluble in water too and so could not be collected in the way Hales had devised. In order to try and collect water-soluble gases, he replaced water with mercury. This made it possible for him to collect the gases now called sulphur dioxide and ammonia.

Priestley was given a large lens called a burning glass. It was designed to focus the Sun's rays onto substances to heat them. Priestley began testing the substances in his laboratory with the heat from the burning glass.

*(continued)*

In Priestley's time a substance such as ash which formed after a substance had been heated was called calx. Priestley had some mercury calx from a previous experiment and when he heated it with the burning glass it turned from a red powder to silver globules of the liquid metal. A gas was also produced which Priestley collected and tested. He found that things that burned in air burned more strongly in this new gas.

Priestley believed in the phlogiston theory and he explained that substances burned so well in this gas because they rapidly lost their phlogiston to it. For this to happen, Priestley believed that the gas did not have any phlogiston and he called it dephlogisticated air.

**Figure C**   Joseph Priestley.

### The end of the phlogiston theory

Antoine Lavoisier (1743–1794) believed in making measurements in his experiments. He discovered that when he heated metals such as lead or tin in a sealed container the metal calxes weighed more than the original metals and that the volume of the air after heating had decreased by about a fifth.

In 1774 Priestley met Lavoisier and told him about his discovery of dephlogisticated air. Lavoisier repeated Priestley's experiments and realised that the dephlogisticated air was the part of the air that combined with the metals to form calxes. He named this gas oxygen. The phlogisticated air which made up the other four fifths of the air became known as nitrogen.

Lavoisier reasoned that when the metals were heated in air they combined with oxygen in the air and that was why their calxes increased in weight and the volume of the air decreased. The phlogiston theory could not account for the change in weight and chemists finally realised that phlogiston did not exist. They realised that when chemical reactions take place it is *matter* that moves.

1  Which discoveries did not easily fit in with the phlogiston theory?
2  What contribution did Stephen Hales make to the study of gases?
3  How did Black's work change the way chemists thought about gases?
4  How did Priestley's discovery of dephlogisticated air fit in with Lavoisier's observations about
  a)  the reduction in the volume of air when it is heated with a metal,
  b)  the change in weight when the calx formed?
5  What do we now believe happens when lead or tin is heated in air?

# Action of oxygen on some metal surfaces

When aluminium, zinc or chromium are exposed to the air they react with the oxygen in it and a very thin layer of the metal oxide forms on their surfaces. The layer prevents more oxygen in the air reacting with the metal and the metal is protected from any further change.

## Rust

When water vapour from the air condenses on iron or steel it forms a film on the surface of the metal. Oxygen dissolves in the water and reacts with the metal to form iron oxide. This forms brown flakes of rust which break off from the surface and expose more metal to the oxygen dissolved in the water. The iron or steel continues to produce rust until it has completely corroded. Steel is used for making girders that support bridges and for making many parts of cars. If the steel is not protected it soon begins to rust. This weakens the metal. It makes bridges unsafe. It makes holes in car bodies and weakens the joints that hold the car together, making them unsafe for use.

**Figure 7.12** A rusted gate post.

**8** Many tall buildings have a framework made of steel girders on which walls of brick and glass are built. If the steel was unprotected what would you expect to happen in time? Explain your answer.

## *Rust prevention*

Rust can be prevented by keeping oxygen away from the iron or steel surface. This can be done by painting the surface or covering it in oil. However, if the paint becomes chipped or the oil is allowed to dry up, rust can begin to form. Steel can also be protected by covering the surface with chromium in a process called chromium plating. Steel used for canning foods is coated in a thin layer of tin.

The steel used for girders to build office blocks and bridges is coated in zinc in a process called galvanising or zinc plating (see also Chapter 10).

# Controlling food spoilage

Oxygen in the air reacts with molecules of fat in food and makes the food smell and taste bad. The food is inedible. Food can be prevented from spoiling in this way by using vacuum packaging to remove as much air as possible from around the food, replacing the air around the food with nitrogen, or adding antioxidants to the food which prevent the reaction with oxygen from taking place.

## ◆ SUMMARY ◆

◆ The atmosphere is divided into five layers *(see page 77)*.
◆ Nitrogen, oxygen and the noble gases in the air have their uses *(see page 79)*.
◆ Burning is a type of combustion in which a flame is produced *(see page 82)*.
◆ Incomplete combustion can be dangerous *(see page 84)*.
◆ The Bunsen burner is a device which allows the combustion of methane to be controlled to supply heat for experiments *(see page 84)*.
◆ A study of the triangle of fire helps in the understanding of how fires can be controlled *(see page 85)*.
◆ Oxygen forms an oxide layer on some metals and is needed for iron and steel to rust *(see page 89)*.
◆ Some foods can be prevented from spoiling by keeping them away from oxygen or by adding antioxidants *(see page 90)*.

## *End of chapter question*

**1** Air is a useful raw material for the chemical industry but it can also create problems. Assess the truth of this statement and give examples to support your ideas.

# 8 The Earth – a rocky planet

A pebble or a stone seems a permanent object – one that has not changed through time. This is not true. Rocks form and change like many other substances but these changes can take millions of years.

Pebbles and stones form from materials inside the Earth that become changed as they spend time near or on the Earth's surface. Eventually they may return to the inside and complete the rock cycle. By the end of this chapter you should be able to trace the path of rocky material as it forms different types of rock and follows the rock cycle.

The Earth is a rocky planet like Mercury, Venus, Mars and Pluto. By studying how the Earth shakes during earthquakes we know how the materials inside the Earth are arranged.

**Figure 8.1** The shape of this rocky mountain is constantly changing.

## The Earth's structure

The core is divided into an inner and an outer core. The inner core is a ball of iron and nickel which is 2740 km in diameter. There are radioactive materials like uranium present, and the heat that they generate keeps the core temperature at about 5000°C. The metals in the inner core still remain solid even though the temperature is above their normal melting point. The great pressure of the other materials in the planet pushing on them prevents them from turning from a solid into a liquid.

The outer core is 2000 km thick and is composed of more iron and nickel. The two metals in this layer are in liquid form. As the Earth turns, the inner core moves at a different speed from the outer core and this difference in movement of the two metallic regions is thought to generate the Earth's magnetic field.

The mantle is made of rocky material, 2900 km thick and is composed mainly of the elements iron, silicon, oxygen and magnesium. The oxygen is combined with silicon to make compounds called silicates. The mantle is very hot, for example, it is 1500°C at a depth of 2000 km below the Earth's surface. Although this is above the normal melting point of the rock, the pressure of the materials above the rock keep it solid. The upper mantle near the crust is cooler and is under less pressure. It behaves like a very thick liquid and flows a little like toothpaste does when you gently squeeze the tube.

The rocky material in the mantle is made of crystals. In certain places in the upper mantle the pressure is reduced. This allows the hot rock to melt. The molten rock or magma is lighter than the solid rock and flows upwards between the crystals. As the magma rises it takes heat with it – melting the rocks it touches. The magma can travel upwards through the Earth's crust and reach the surface (see Volcanoes page 93).

1  Why is the centre of the Earth hot?

2  If you could travel from the centre of the Earth to its surface how would the temperature change?

3  What is magma and why does it reach the Earth's surface?

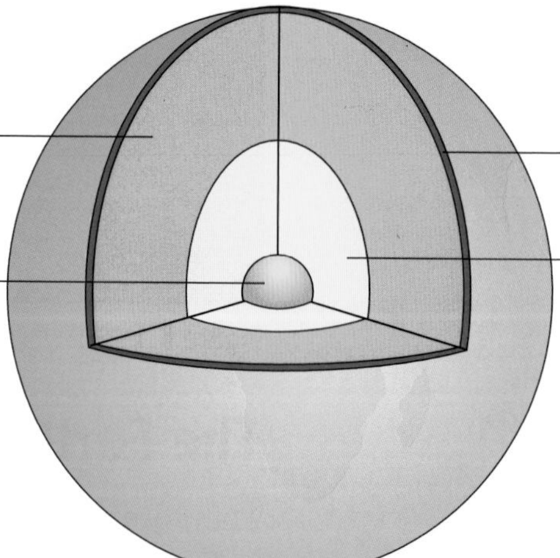

**Figure 8.2**  The solid structure of the Earth (atmosphere and water excluded).

## The Earth's crust

The Earth's crust is made from much cooler rocks than the mantle. Although rocks at the surface feel cold, miners and cavers can feel an increase in temperature as they go down into the ground.

There are two kinds of crust – the oceanic crust and the continental crust. The oceanic crust is about 8 km thick and is made of a rock called basalt. The continental crust is between 20 and 70 km thick and is mainly made of a rock called granite.

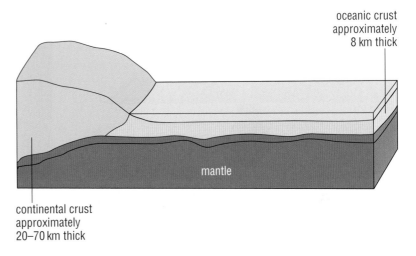

**Figure 8.3**   The two kinds of crust – oceanic and continental.

# Volcanoes

A volcano is a mountain made from molten rock and ash that has come from below the Earth's surface. There are two main kinds of volcano – the andesitic volcano and the basaltic volcano.

## *Andesitic volcanoes*

This type of volcano is named after the Andes mountains in South America where the form was first identified. Andesitic volcanoes form cone-shaped mountains above the ground. Inside the volcano is a tube called a vent. The magma passes through the vent to the surface.

After an eruption, ash settles in the vent and blocks it. When the magma collects beneath the volcano again it pushes on the ash. Water in the magma escapes as steam and also pushes on the ash. Eventually, the pressure becomes so great that the ash is pushed upwards and the walls of the vent are then pushed outwards in a huge explosion.

Pieces of rock the size of houses are flung down the sides of the volcano. Dust, ash and lumps of molten rock, called pyroclastic bombs, shoot into the air and thick, sticky lava flows out of the vent and moves slowly down the sides of the volcano.

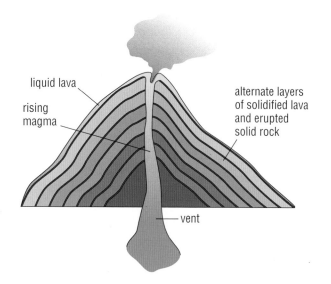

liquid lava

rising
magma

alternate layers
of solidified lava
and erupted
solid rock

vent

**Figure 8.4** Structure and eruption of an andesitic volcano.

## *Basaltic volcanoes*

Most basaltic volcanoes are on the ocean bed. They are flatter than the andesitic volcanoes and are sometimes called shield volcanoes. They form over areas of the mantle called hot spots. In a hot spot, the pressure on the rock in the mantle is reduced and it melts and rises. The molten rock forms a much thinner lava than in an andesitic volcano. It does not block the shield volcano's vent or build up pressure. The lava runs away and spreads out over a large area. It forms a black rock called basalt. Where basaltic volcanoes are formed on land their eruptions are usually much less violent than those of andesitic volcanoes and scientists can get quite close to study them.

**4** The eruption of a large volcano may alter the colour of the sunsets around the world. How may this happen?

**5** How are andesitic and basaltic volcanoes **a)** similar, **b)** different?

**6** Pumice is a rock with holes in it. It floats on water. How may it have been formed when a volcano erupted?

**Figure 8.5** A basaltic volcano erupting in Hawaii, USA.

# Types of rock

## Igneous rock

There are two kinds of igneous or fire rocks and they both form from molten rock. Igneous rock that reaches the Earth's surface is called extrusive igneous rock. It forms from molten rock in the mantle that reaches the Earth's surface through a volcano.

Igneous rock that does not reach the Earth's surface straight away is called intrusive igneous rock. It forms from molten rock that cools and turns into a solid in the Earth's crust.

Basalt is an example of an extrusive igneous rock. It cools quickly in the air at the Earth's surface and then forms a structure made of small crystals.

Granite is an example of an intrusive igneous rock. It forms from molten rock in the crust. Granite does not reach the Earth's surface and cools slowly in the crust to form a structure featuring large crystals.

**Figure 8.6** Basalt (left) and granite (right) – the crystals in the basalt are too small to be seen easily but the crystals of the different minerals in granite can be clearly seen.

## *Uses of igneous rock*

Granite and basalt are very hard and so are used to make foundations and surfaces for roads and for making concrete.

Basalt is used to form the protective shielding in nuclear power stations that prevents the escape of harmful radiation.

The different shapes and colours of its crystals make the polished, smooth surface of granite very attractive. It is used for decorative stonework on the front entrances to important buildings such as museums and libraries.

**7** Why do you think igneous rocks are called fire rocks?

**8** What is the difference between an extrusive and an intrusive igneous rock? Give an example of each kind.

**9** How could you tell an extrusive rock from an intrusive rock?

**10** What property of granite makes it useful for **a)** making roads, **b)** forming the doorway to a library?

**Figure 8.7**  The granite entrance to a building.

# Minerals

A mineral is a substance which has formed from one or more elements in the Earth. Gold, silver and copper are examples of the very few elements that are found on their own. When an element is found alone it is called a native element. Most other minerals are compounds.

Table 8.1 shows the ten most common elements in the Earth's crust. Most minerals are made of compounds that contain one or more of these elements. For example, quartz is made of a compound of silicon and oxygen.

The atoms of the elements in a mineral are joined together to form a crystal structure. Each mineral can be recognised by observing its crystal shape, colour, lustre, hardness and the colour of the streak it makes when it is rubbed across a rough, white porcelain surface. Over 2000 minerals have been identified.

Some rarer minerals have particularly attractive properties. They have a pleasing colour, a shiny surface or sparkle when light passes through them. These minerals such as opal, diamond and beryl (which is cut to form emeralds) are called gemstones. Different gemstones may be formed in different ways. For example, diamond forms in hot rock which rises through the Earth's crust. Beryl forms in the last part of granite rock to cool in the crust and opal forms from the minerals dissolved in the water of hot springs or from the weathering of certain kinds of rock.

1  What is a mineral?
2  Make a key to identify the five pieces of quartz in Figure A.
3  What are the properties of gemstones?
4  Are gemstones minerals? Explain your answer.

**Table 8.1**

| Element | % in crust |
|---------|------------|
| Oxygen | 50 |
| Silicon | 25.8 |
| Aluminium | 7.3 |
| Iron | 4.2 |
| Calcium | 3.2 |
| Sodium | 2.4 |
| Potassium | 2.3 |
| Magnesium | 2.0 |
| Hydrogen | 1.0 |
| Titanium | 0.4 |

*(continued)*

Rock crystal

Rose quartz

Smoky quartz

Milky quartz

Amethyst

**Figure A**   Varieties of quartz .

## Sedimentary rock

Sedimentary rocks are formed from particles which have settled out at the bottom of a river, lake or sea. There are three kinds of sedimentary rock.

- The particles in one kind have been produced by weathering. They were carried down rivers and settled out when the water current slowed down. Over long periods of time – thousands or even millions of years – the layers of particles built up. As the thickness and the weight of the layers increased the particles became squashed together. In time the different particles bound together to make a firm rock. Sandstone is a good example of this type of sedimentary rock (see Figure 8.8).
- Another kind is made up from particles of living things. Limestone is formed from the shells of sea creatures such as molluscs that collect at the bottom of the sea. Chalk forms from the tiny shells of protoctists which lived in the plankton of ancient seas (see Figure 8.8).

- The last kind, for example rock salt and gypsum, form when a sea dries up. As the water evaporates the remaining sea water becomes more concentrated. Eventually, there is too little water left for all the chemicals to remain in solution and they combine to form crystals.

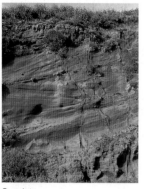
Sandstone

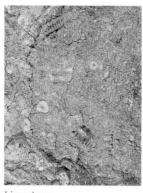
Limestone

Chalk

Rock salt

**Figure 8.8** Types of sedimentary rock.

## *Uses of sedimentary rock*

Sandstone and limestone form layers called beds. The place where the different beds meet is weaker than the surrounding rock and allows the rock to be easily broken up into pieces that are the right size to be used as building stone.

Limestone has many uses in the chemical industry. Rock salt is also used in the chemical industry and for spreading on roads in winter. It dissolves in the water on the road and lowers its freezing point, preventing the formation of ice on which traffic could skid. Gypsum is used in making cement and plaster.

## Metamorphic rock

These rocks are formed from igneous or sedimentary rocks that have been heated or squashed in the Earth's crust. The pressure and the rise in temperature cause the rocks to change their form, or metamorphose. There are two kinds of metamorphic rock.

- One kind occurs around intrusions of igneous rock into the crust. The hot igneous rock heats the surrounding rocks in the crust to 700–1100°C. The rise in temperature can cause the mineral crystals to melt and then recrystallise into new minerals. Marble is an example of a metamorphic rock that forms when limestone is heated in this way (see Figure 8.9).

**11** Compare the ways in which the different kinds of sedimentary rock are formed.

**12** Why are sandstone and limestone frequently used as building stone?

- The other kind is produced when rocks in the crust are squashed together during the formation of mountains. The pressure causes the rocks to become hot. Slate forms in this way from a rock called shale. Shale is a sedimentary rock with very tiny particles similar to those in clay and mud. Slate is also made of tiny particles or grains but when the rock is struck it breaks up into thin sheets (see Figure 8.9).

**Figure 8.9** Marble (left) and slate (right).

**13** What does metamorphosis mean?

**14** What causes a rock to metamorphose?

**15** Limestone is a grey rock with a rough powdery texture. What does it become after it has metamorphosed? What properties does the new rock have?

**16** How do the properties of slate make it useful for a roofing material?

## *Uses of metamorphic rock*

The glistening, sugar-like texture of marble and its streaks of colourful minerals make marble an attractive rock. It is used to make statues for staircases and entrances in important buildings such as town halls and also for the tops of expensive and decorative tables.

Slate is non-porous (it does not let water through) and forms lightweight sheets. In the past, these properties made it a useful roofing material and many old buildings still have slate roofs. New buildings are roofed in clay tiles. Slate has a very smooth surface, which is why it is used to support the green cover of billiard tables.

# How rock breaks up

All rocks exposed at the Earth's surface are broken up over a long time by a process called weathering. There are two kinds of weathering – physical weathering and chemical weathering.

## Physical weathering

A rock can suffer physical weathering in several ways. In a gale, grit and sand grains carried in the wind rub and scratch the surface of the rock as they blow against it. These fast moving particles chip pieces off the rock surface and change its shape.

During the heat of the day the rock expands. At night it cools down and contracts. Expansion and contraction generate pushing and pulling forces in the rock structure and weaken it.

Water may be soaked up by some rocks, such as sandstone or limestone, or it may collect in the cracks of almost any rock. In cold weather the water freezes and expands. The forces generated by the ice cause pieces of rock to snap off.

**Figure 8.10** A scree slope formed by physical weathering.

The fragments of rock produced by physical weathering may be blown away in the wind to cause weathering to other rocks or be washed into streams, rivers, lakes and seas to form sedimentary rocks. Some particles form part of the soil.

**17** How may a grain of sand have been formed?

## Chemical weathering

This occurs in rocks such as limestone that contain compounds such as calcium carbonate and magnesium carbonate. These compounds can be attacked by acids and washed away from the rock.

Carbon dioxide dissolves in the water droplets in a cloud or rain to make a weakly acidic solution. This solution reacts with the carbonates in limestone and causes holes to develop in the rock. These holes may become very large and are called pot holes.

Sulphur dioxide from industrial smoke dissolves in water to form sulphuric acid, a major component of acid rain. When sulphuric acid attacks the rock, calcium and magnesium sulphates form. They form crystals in the spaces in the rock as it dries out and the crystals push on the structure of the rock. After the rock has been soaked with acid rain and dried out many times, the strain created by the sulphate crystals causes part of the rock to crumble.

**18** Where do pot holes form?

**19** How is the chemical weathering caused by the acid produced when carbon dioxide dissolves in rain water, different from that caused by acid rain produced by sulphur dioxide?

**Figure 8.11**   The middle stone face, which has been damaged by acid rain, has yet to be replaced.

# Completing the rock cycle

The way rocks form and are destroyed makes a cycle. Part of the rock cycle can be worked out in the following way.

Igneous rocks come from molten rock (magma) in the mantle and the crust and are exposed at the Earth's surface. The rock is weathered and broken down into fragments which settle out into layers and form sedimentary rock. In time, the sedimentary and igneous rocks may be squashed and heated and may change to metamorphic rock.

The link that is missing is the one between the metamorphic rocks in the crust and the magma. The clue to the link is in the squashing of the rocks to make metamorphic rocks. Squashing suggests that they move together. It has been discovered that the crust is divided into huge plates which are moved by the actions of the upper mantle.

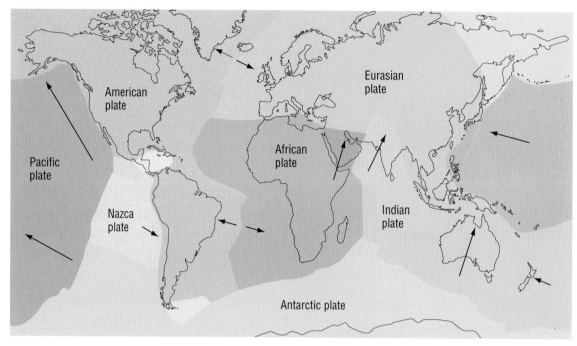

**Figure 8.12** Plates in the Earth's mantle. The arrows show the direction of plate movement.

The mantle moves a plate in one direction. As the plate moves, new material is added at the place it leaves behind. At the opposite edge, the plate is pushing into another plate and its material is sinking into the mantle.

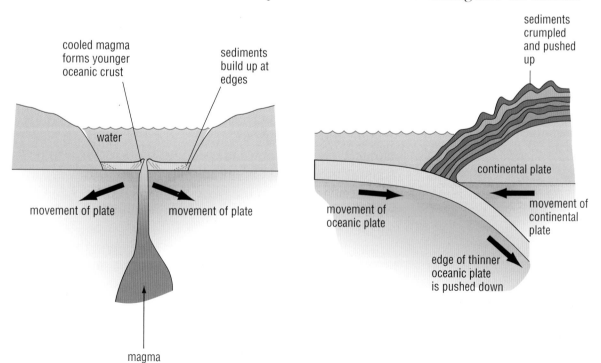

**Figure 8.13** The oceanic and continental plates colliding.

**20** Construct a rock cycle featuring the recycling of sedimentary rock.

**21** Amphibolite is formed from basalt that has been heated up when rocks are squashed during mountain building. How can you use this information to add another arrow to the rock cycle?

These movements account for the squashing of the rocks to form mountains and the formation of magma in andesitic volcanoes. Basaltic volcanoes provide the new rock at the other edge of the plate.

The discoveries about the plates can be used to complete a rock cycle as shown in Figure 8.14.

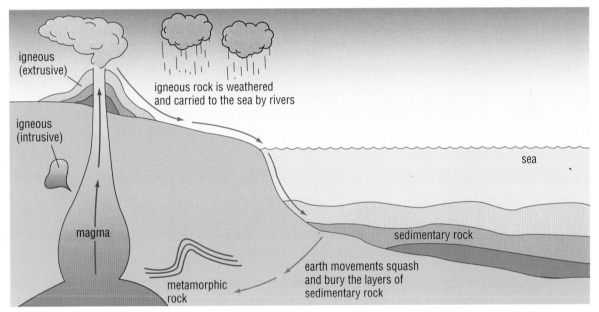

**Figure 8.14** The rock cycle.

# ◆ SUMMARY ◆

◆ Igneous rock forms from molten rock beneath the Earth's crust *(see page 95)*.

◆ Sedimentary rocks form in a variety of ways *(see page 97)*.

◆ Metamorphic rock is produced by the action of heat or pressure on rocks inside the Earth *(see page 98)*.

◆ Rocks on the Earth's surface are broken up by a process called weathering *(see page 99)*.

## *End of chapter question*

**1** A building has a slate roof, granite walls, a marble floor and a sandstone doorway. What processes took place to form these different kinds of building materials?

# 9 Metals and non-metals

Elements can be divided into two large groups, according to their properties. These groups are called metals and non-metals.

## Physical properties

Table 9.1 shows the physical properties of the elements in the two groups.

**Table 9.1** The physical properties of metals and non-metals.

| Property | Metal | Non-metal |
|---|---|---|
| state at room temperature | solid | solid, liquid or gas |
| density | high | low |
| surface | shiny | dull |
| melting point | generally high | generally low |
| boiling point | generally high | generally low |
| effect of hammering | shaped without breaking | breaks easily |
| effect of tapping | a ringing sound | no ringing sound |
| strength | high | generally very weak |
| magnetic | a few examples | no examples |
| conduction of heat | good | poor |
| conduction of electricity | good | poor |

A material through which electricity can pass is called an electrical conductor. A material through which electricity cannot pass is called an insulator.

A material through which heat can pass is called a conductor of heat. A material through which heat cannot pass is called an insulator.

Non-metals have a wider range of physical properties than metals because nearly all metals are solid at room temperature and non-metals can either be solids, liquids or gases.

Using physical properties to group elements can be unreliable as a few elements have exceptional properties. Mercury is the only metal that is a liquid at normal room temperature, and iodine is a solid with a shiny surface that looks metallic even though it is a non-metal.

Carbon is an element that can exist in different crystalline forms. Each form is called an allotrope of the element. Two allotropes of carbon are graphite and diamond. Diamond has a very high melting point and boiling point, while graphite conducts electricity. Metals and non-metals can be more clearly identified by their chemical properties.

**1** Why may physical properties be unreliable for grouping substances into metals and non-metals?

**Figure 9.1** Diamond (left) and graphite (right).

# Chemical properties

Some metals and non-metals react together to produce salts. These reactions are examples of synthesis reactions (see page 64). For example, if a burning piece of sodium is placed in a jar of chlorine gas in a fume cupboard the two elements combine to make a white solid. The word equation for this reaction is:

sodium + chlorine → sodium chloride

If zinc or copper are heated with sulphur the metal sulphides are formed. The word equations for these reactions are:

zinc + sulphur → zinc sulphide

copper + sulphur → copper sulphide

Oxygen is a non-metal and reacts with many metals and non-metals to form oxides.

## Reaction with oxygen

If a metal takes part in a chemical reaction with oxygen, a metal oxide is formed. A metal oxide is a base (see page 71) and forms a salt and water when it takes part in a chemical reaction with an acid. A few metal oxides are soluble in water. They are called alkalis. Calcium oxide is a soluble base (an alkali). This is the reaction that occurs with calcium oxide and water:

calcium oxide + water → calcium hydroxide

If a non-metal takes part in a chemical reaction with oxygen it also forms an oxide. Most oxides of non-metals are soluble. When they dissolve in water they form acids. Sulphur is a non-metallic element with a yellow crystalline form. If it is heated in air it burns and combines with oxygen to form sulphur dioxide, which is soluble in water. This reaction occurs between sulphur dioxide and water:

$$\text{sulphur dioxide} + \text{water} \rightarrow \text{sulphurous acid}$$

When carbon powder is heated in air it glows red. If it is plunged into a gas jar of oxygen it becomes bright red. Carbon combines with oxygen to form carbon dioxide, which dissolves in water to form an acidic solution with a pH of 5.

Magnesium ribbon easily catches fire if it is held in a Bunsen burner flame and burns with a brilliant white light if plunged into a gas jar of oxygen. Magnesium oxide (a white powder) is produced, which dissolves in water to make an alkaline solution with a pH of 8.

**2** How may the reaction with oxygen be used to distinguish a metal from a non-metal?

**3** Use the information in this section to decide whether **a)** carbon, and **b)** magnesium is a metal or a non-metal. Explain your answer.

# The periodic table

The periodic table (see also Chapter 13) is used to arrange the elements in order, based on the structure of their atoms. It can also be used to locate metallic and non-metallic elements (see below).

1 H hydrogen

metals

non-metals

| I | II | | | | | | | | | | | III | IV | V | VI | VII | VIII |
|---|---|---|---|---|---|---|---|---|---|---|---|---|---|---|---|---|---|
| | | | | | | | | | | | | | | | | | 2 He helium |
| 3 Li lithium | 4 Be beryllium | | | | | | | | | | | 5 B boron | 6 C carbon | 7 N nitrogen | 8 O oxygen | 9 F fluorine | 10 Ne neon |
| 11 Na sodium | 12 Mg magnesium | | | | | | | | | | | 13 Al aluminium | 14 Si silicon | 15 P phosphorus | 16 S sulphur | 17 Cl chlorine | 18 Ar argon |
| 19 K potassium | 20 Ca calcium | 21 Sc scandium | 22 Ti titanium | 23 V vanadium | 24 Cr chromium | 25 Mn manganese | 26 Fe iron | 27 Co cobalt | 28 Ni nickel | 29 Cu copper | 30 Zn zinc | 31 Ga gallium | 32 Ge germanium | 33 As arsenic | 34 Se selenium | 35 Br bromine | 36 Kr krypton |
| 37 Rb rubidium | 38 Sr strontium | 39 Y yttrium | 40 Zr zirconium | 41 Nb niobium | 42 Mo molybdenum | 43 Tc technetium | 44 Ru ruthenium | 45 Rh rhodium | 46 Pd palladium | 47 Ag silver | 48 Cd cadmium | 49 In indium | 50 Sn tin | 51 Sb antimony | 52 Te tellurium | 53 I iodine | 54 Xe xenon |
| 55 Cs caesium | 56 Ba barium | | 72 Hf hafnium | 73 Ta tantalum | 74 W tungsten | 75 Re rhenium | 76 Os osmium | 77 Ir iridium | 78 Pt platinum | 79 Au gold | 80 Hg mercury | 81 Tl thallium | 82 Pb lead | 83 Bi bismuth | 84 Po polonium | 85 At astatine | 86 Rn radon |

**Figure 9.2** The periodic table, showing the metallic and non-metallic division.

# A closer look at metals

Metals have different physical properties such as colour, hardness and density that allow us to tell them apart. Metals also behave differently from each other when they come into contact with oxygen, water, acids and the salts of other metals. By studying the way the metals react, a 'league table' called the reactivity series can be constructed with the most reactive metals at the top and the least reactive metals at the bottom.

## Reaction with oxygen

Here are some descriptions of the reactions that take place when certain metals are heated with oxygen.

Copper develops a covering of a black powder without glowing or bursting into flame. Iron glows and produces yellow sparks; a black powder is left behind. Sodium only needs a little heat to make it burst into yellow flames and burn quickly to leave a yellow powder behind (see Figure 9.3). Gold is not changed after it has been heated then left to cool.

**4** Arrange the metals mentioned opposite in order of their reactivity with oxygen. Start with what you consider to be the most reactive metal.

**Figure 9.3** Sodium burning in a gas jar of oxygen (left). Sodium oxide powder is left behind (right).

## Reaction with water

Here are some descriptions of the reactions that take place between water and metals. In the study of these reactions the metals were first tested with cold water. If there was no reaction, the test was repeated with steam (see Figure 9.4).

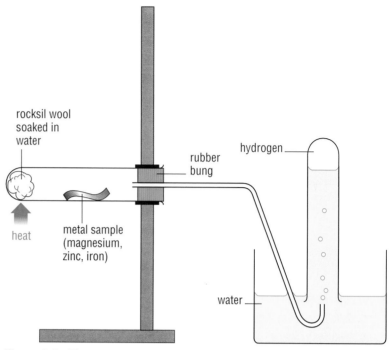

**Figure 9.4**   The apparatus to test the action of steam on a metal.

5 Arrange the metals in this section (including those at the top of page 109) in order of their reactivity with water.

6 Which metals would not be put into the apparatus in Figure 9.4 to see if they reacted with steam?

7 Which metals are less dense than water?

8 Water is a compound of hydrogen and oxygen which could be called hydrogen oxide. When hydrogen is released as a metal reacts with steam, what do you think is the other product of the reaction?

9 In the home, copper is used for the hot water tank and steel (a modified form of iron – see page 129) is used to make the cold water tank. Why can steel not be used to make the hot water tank?

Calcium sinks in cold water and bubbles of hydrogen form on its surface, slowly at first. The bubbles then increase in number quickly and the water becomes cloudy as calcium hydroxide forms. The bubbles of gas can be collected by placing a test-tube filled with water over the fizzing metal. The gas pushes the water out of the test-tube. If the tube, now filled with gas, is quickly raised out of the water and a lighted splint held beneath its mouth, a popping sound is heard. The hydrogen in the tube combines with oxygen in the air and this explosive reaction makes the popping sound.

Copper sinks in cold water and does not react with it. Neither does it react with steam.

Sodium floats on the surface of water and a fizzing sound is heard as bubbles of hydrogen gas are quickly produced around it. The production of the gas may push the metal across the water surface and against the side of the container, where the metal bursts into flame. A clear solution of sodium hydroxide forms.

Iron sinks in water and no bubbles of hydrogen form. When the metal is heated in steam, hydrogen is produced slowly.

Magnesium sinks in water. Bubbles of hydrogen are produced only very slowly and a solution of magnesium hydroxide is formed. When the metal is heated in steam hydrogen is produced quickly.

Potassium floats on water and bursts into flames immediately. Hydrogen bubbles are rapidly produced around the metal. A clear solution of potassium hydroxide forms.

## Reaction with acids

Here are some descriptions of the reactions that take place between different metals and hydrochloric acid. The metals were first tested with dilute hydrochloric acid. If a reaction did not take place, they were tested with concentrated hydrochloric acid.

Lead did not react with dilute hydrochloric acid but when tested with concentrated acid, bubbles of hydrogen gas were produced slowly and a solution of lead chloride was formed.

Zinc reacted quite slowly with dilute hydrochloric acid to produce bubbles of hydrogen and a solution of zinc chloride was formed.

Copper did not react with either dilute or concentrated hydrochloric acid.

Magnesium reacted quickly with dilute hydrochloric acid and formed bubbles of hydrogen and a solution of magnesium chloride.

Iron reacted slowly with dilute hydrochloric acid to produce bubbles of hydrogen and a solution of iron chloride was formed.

**10** Arrange the metals in order of reactivity with hydrochloric acid.

**11** Why was a concentrated solution used if there was no reaction with a dilute solution?

**12** If a metal which had reacted very slowly with a dilute acid was tested with a concentrated one, what would you predict would happen?

**13** Construct a general word equation for the reaction between a metal and hydrochloric acid. (Instead of using the name of a metal, just use the word 'metal' instead.)

**Figure 9.5** The reaction of magnesium with dilute hydrochloric acid produces hydrogen bubbles.

## Displacement reactions

(See also Chapter 5 page 65.)

When metals react with acids, they displace hydrogen from the acid and form a salt solution. In a similar way, a more reactive metal can displace a less reactive metal from a salt solution of the metal.

When a copper wire is suspended in a solution of silver sulphate, the copper dissolves into the solution to form copper sulphate and silver metal comes out of the solution and settles on the wire (see Figure 9.6).

**Figure 9.6**  Copper wire coils in silver sulphate solution. Silver is formed on the wire.

**14** From the information about these two displacement reactions, arrange the three metals in order of reactivity – starting with the most reactive.

If an iron nail is placed in copper sulphate solution, the iron dissolves to form a pale green iron sulphate solution and the copper comes out of the solution and coats the nail (see Figure 9.7).

**Figure 9.7**  This iron nail has been left in copper sulphate solution. Copper has formed on the nail.

Look at Table 9.2 opposite to answer these questions.

**15** How do you think the reactions that zinc makes with oxygen, water and acid compare with those that iron makes?

**16** From Table 9.2, would you expect zinc to displace
**a)** iron, **b)** lead,
**c)** aluminium in displacement reactions? Explain your answers.

## The reactivity series

The reactivity series is a list of metals arranged in order of their reactivity, starting with the most reactive. The series is produced by studying the reactions of metals with oxygen, water, hydrochloric acid and solutions of metal salts. Table 9.2 shows 12 metals in the reactivity series and summarises their reactions with oxygen, water and hydrochloric acid.

**Table 9.2**  The reactivity series.

| Metal | Reaction with oxygen | Reaction with water | Reaction with acid |
|---|---|---|---|
| potassium | oxide forms very vigorously | produces hydrogen with cold water | violent reaction |
| sodium | | | |
| calcium | | produces hydrogen with steam | rate of reaction decreases down the table |
| magnesium | | | |
| aluminium | | | |
| zinc | | | |
| iron | oxide forms slowly | | |
| tin | oxide forms without burning | no reaction with water or steam | very slow reaction |
| lead | | | |
| copper | | | no reaction |
| silver | no reaction | | |
| gold | | | |

# Generating electricity with metals

Chemical reactions between metals are used to generate electricity on a small scale. Electricity is generated on a large scale by making use of the magnetic properties of metals.

When two strips of copper are suspended in a solution of sodium chloride, the light emitting diode (LED) does not light up. If the LED is replaced by a voltmeter the needle remains at zero – showing that there is no electricity flowing.

**17** What is the LED used for in the circuit?

**18** Here are the readings from the voltmeter when pairs of different metals are tested in sodium chloride solution:

> iron and copper   0.7
> magnesium and copper  −2.7
> iron and lead   0.3

Look at the reactivity series and identify a relationship between the pairs of metals and the size of the voltage between them.

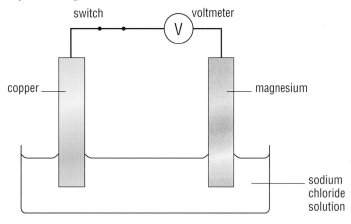

**Figure 9.8**  Copper and magnesium strips in sodium chloride solution.

If a strip of magnesium is put in place of one of the copper strips the LED lights up and if a voltmeter is used in the circuit, as shown in Figure 9.8, the needles swings away from the zero mark.

## The dry cell

The structure of a dry cell is shown in Figure 9.9. Dry cells are used in a torch. When the torch is switched on, the zinc atoms on the inner surface of the casing lose their electrons and the electrons flow through the circuit in the torch and the bulb lights. When the electrons reach the carbon rod they enter the paste, where complicated chemical reactions take place to prevent the build-up of hydrogen bubbles on the rod surface. These reactions allow the electrons to flow round the circuit.

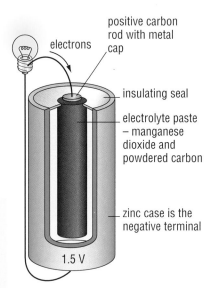

electrons

positive carbon rod with metal cap

insulating seal

electrolyte paste – manganese dioxide and powdered carbon

zinc case is the negative terminal

1.5 V

**Figure 9.9** Inside a zinc–carbon dry cell.

**19** What are the advantages of using a dry cell instead of one containing a liquid?

**20** Why do you think a dry cell eventually stops working?

# How electricity came to be used in chemistry

Joseph Priestley (1733–1804) (see also page 87) spent some time studying electricity. He discovered that carbon conducted electricity, examined the work of other scientists on electricity and wrote a book about their research.

Alessandro Volta (1745–1827) was an Italian scientist who became interested in electricity after reading Priestley's book. He also studied the work of Luigi Galvani (1737–1798) who believed that he had discovered 'animal electricity'. Galvani studied how human and animal bodies were constructed, but he also had a machine which generated static electricity in his laboratory. He discovered that when the machine was working, the muscles in dissected frogs' legs twitched. He also discovered that the muscles twitched when they touched two different metals – such as copper and iron. From his observations, he concluded that the muscles contained electricity.

**Figure A** Luigi Galvani

*(continued)*

Volta believed that the muscles were not important in the generation of electricity and replaced them with a salt solution. He arranged a row of bowls of salt solution with strips of copper and zinc dipping into each one. The bowls with their metal strips were joined together and were called a battery. It was the first device made that could produce a steady flow of electric current. Later, Volta re-designed his battery into a pile of copper and zinc discs. The copper and zinc discs were separated by cardboard that had been soaked in salt solution. This device became known as the voltaic pile (see Figure B).

**Figure B**   Volta demonstrates his battery to Napoleon.

Volta wrote to the Royal Society in London about his invention so that other scientists could learn how to construct it. When William Nicholson (1753–1815) and Anthony Carlisle (1768–1840) constructed a voltaic pile, they connected it to two pieces of metal that were dipping into water. Bubbles of gas were produced on the metal pieces. The bubbles on one piece of metal contained hydrogen, and the bubbles on the other piece of metal contained oxygen.

Humphry Davy (1778–1829) was an English chemist. He realised that Nicholson and Carlisle's discovery that electricity could split up a substance into its elements could be more widely used. At the time, substances such as potash and lime were thought to be compounds of elements but reactions with other chemicals could not split them up.

Davy built a very large battery, heated each substance until it melted, then let the current flow through it. When Davy tested potash he discovered tiny pieces of a shiny metal that caught fire when they were placed on water. He had discovered potassium. Look at Table 4.1 on pages 48–50 to see what other elements he discovered.

Michael Faraday (1791–1867) was Davy's assistant but later made a great many discoveries on his own. He gave the name electrolysis to the process of splitting compounds with electricity.

1  How was the work of Priestley linked to the work of Davy?
2  What other conclusion could Galvani have drawn about his work on metals and frogs' legs?
3  Draw how Volta's original battery may have looked. You may draw it in the style of Figure 9.8.
4  How was Volta's pile an improvement on his first battery?
5  Volta's pile showed that a chemical reaction could produce electricity. How do you think scientists like Nicholson and Carlisle might have re-arranged this idea to use electricity in their experiments?
6  What were the elements that Davy discovered?

# Passage of electricity through different substances

A solid can be tested to find out if it conducts electricity by using a circuit like the one shown in Figure 9.10. The solid to be tested is secured between the pair of crocodile clips and the switch is closed. The lamp lights if the solid conducts electricity. By using the circuit, metals and the non-metal carbon, in the form of graphite, are found to conduct electricity. Other non-metals such as sulphur and solid compounds such as sodium chloride do not.

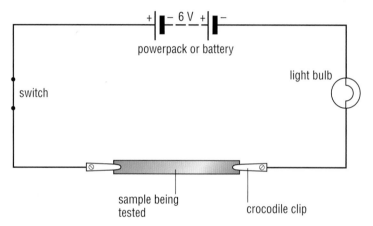

**Figure 9.10**  A circuit for testing conduction of solid materials.

If a liquid is to be tested, the apparatus shown in Figure 9.11 is used. Graphite (carbon) rods are attached to the crocodile clips. The ends of the rods are then lowered into the liquid. A liquid may be a pure liquid or a solution.

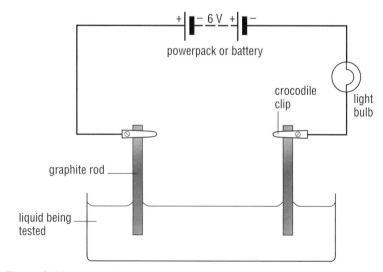

**Figure 9.11**  A circuit for testing conduction of liquids.

## Pure liquids

At room temperature, mercury is a pure liquid that conducts electricity. Ethanol in its pure form does not conduct electricity. Other pure liquids which conduct electricity are formed from compounds such as sodium chloride which have been heated until they melt. Pure water does not conduct electricity but since many substances dissolve readily in it, most water samples are not pure but instead are solutions.

## Solutions

Solutions such as copper sulphate solution and sodium chloride solution, acids such as sulphuric acid and alkalis such as sodium hydroxide solution conduct electricity, but sugar solution does not.

# Electrolysis

Electrolysis is the decomposition of an electrolyte using electricity. An electrolyte is a solution or a molten solid through which the current passes. The elements which are produced as a result of the decomposition collect at the carbon rods. These rods are known as electrodes. Platinum is another material which is used to make electrodes. Carbon and platinum are used because they do not usually take part in chemical reactions with the electrolyte or the chemicals which form on their surfaces. One electrode has a positive charge and is called the anode. The other electrode has a negative charge and is called the cathode.

**21** It is dangerous to touch electrical switches with wet hands. What may have dissolved in the water from sweaty skin that makes it into a conducting solution?

**22** What is an electrolyte? Which substances mentioned under the headings 'Pure liquids' and 'Solutions' are electrolytes?

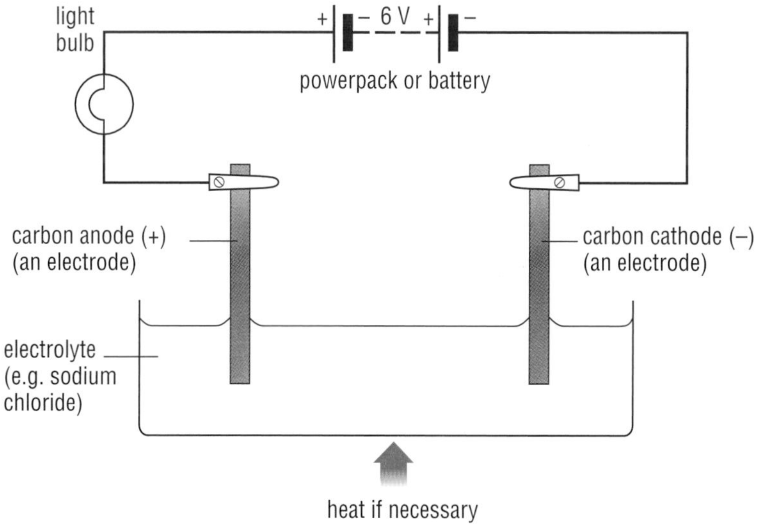

**Figure 9.12**   Apparatus for electrolysis.

## Pure molten electrolyte

When sodium chloride is molten and a current of electricity is passed through it, sodium metal is produced at the cathode and chlorine gas is produced at the anode. (The sodium metal is difficult to see.)

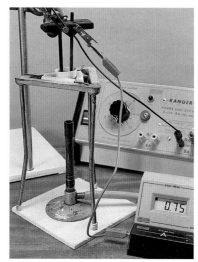

If lead bromide is heated until it melts and a current of electricity is passed through it, an amount of lead is produced at the cathode which is easier to see. Bromine gas is produced at the anode. This experiment should always be performed in a fume cupboard because the bromine gas and lead vapour that escape from the molten electrolyte are toxic.

**Figure 9.13** The electrolysis of lead bromide in a fume cupboard.

## Electrolysis of solutions

### Copper sulphate

When a current of electricity is passed through carbon electrodes in copper sulphate solution, copper metal coats the cathode and oxygen bubbles form on the anode (see Figure 9.14).

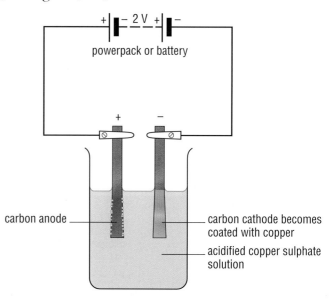

**Figure 9.14** The electrolysis of copper sulphate solution.

## Magnesium sulphate

When a current of electricity is passed through magnesium sulphate solution, bubbles of hydrogen form at the cathode and bubbles of oxygen at the anode (see Figure 9.15).

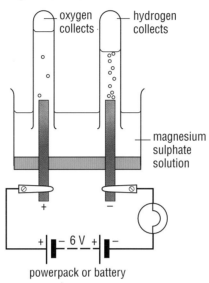

*oxygen collects*
*hydrogen collects*
*magnesium sulphate solution*
*6 V*
powerpack or battery

**Figure 9.15**  The apparatus for collecting two gases by electrolysis.

**23** Which metal described above is **a)** more reactive, **b)** less reactive than hydrogen?

**24** Look at the reactivity series on page 111 and, using your answer to question 23 as a guide, write down the metals you think are **a)** more reactive, and **b)** less reactive than hydrogen.

## Reactivity of hydrogen

The reactivity of hydrogen can be compared with the reactivity of metals. A metal that is less reactive than hydrogen will come out of solution during electrolysis and coat the cathode. A metal which is more reactive than hydrogen will stay in solution and the hydrogen will come out of the solution and form a gas.

# Extraction of metals

## Discovery of reactive metals

Metals at the top of the reactivity series do not occur naturally on their own. They are always combined with other elements to form compounds. Very reactive metals are very difficult to separate from the elements they are combined with in a compound.

When people began to study chemicals scientifically, some compounds were thought to contain unknown elements but the experiments that were used at the time could not split up the compounds. With the invention of a device which could give a steady current of electricity (see page 113), the process of electrolysis was developed and the electrical energy was found to be strong enough to break up the compounds and reveal new metals (see Davy's discoveries in Table 4.1 on pages 48–50).

**25** How do you think that reducing the melting point of an electrolyte makes the metal cheaper to produce?

## Extraction of sodium

The electrolyte is molten sodium chloride. Sodium chloride has a high melting point and requires a large amount of energy to turn it from a solid into a liquid. Calcium chloride is added to the sodium chloride to lower its melting point and reduce the amount of energy required to melt it.

The molten electrolyte is passed into a Down's cell (see Figure 9.16) where sodium is collected from around the steel cathode and chlorine is collected from around the carbon anode.

Electrolysis is also used in the extraction of aluminium (see page 132).

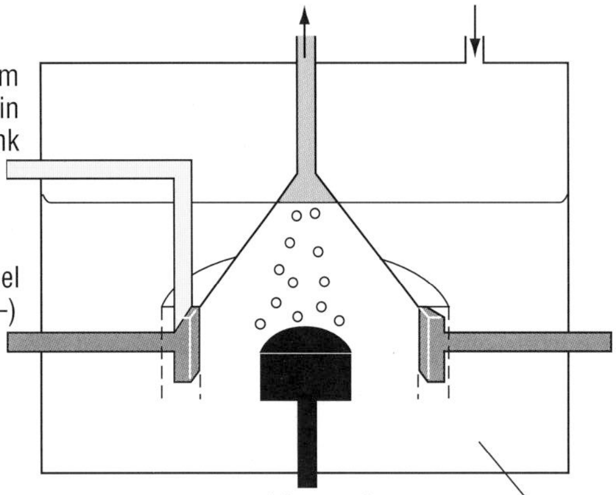

**Figure 9.16** A Down's cell.

## Electrolysis of non-metals

Hydrogen and chlorine are extracted from brine by electrolysis (see Chapter 11 page 143).

## Electroplating

### Plating copper on copper

Two copper electrodes were weighed then dipped into a solution of copper sulphate and the current switched on for half an hour. No bubbles of gas were seen on either electrode and there appeared to be no other changes taking place. At the end of half an hour the current was switched off and the electrodes were cleaned and dried. When the electrodes were re-weighed the cathode was found to have gained weight and the anode was found to have lost weight. The weight lost by the anode was equal to the weight gained by the cathode. Plating copper on copper is used in the purifying of the metal after it has been extracted from its ore (see page 123).

**26** What has happened at the cathode?
**27** What has happened at the anode?

### Plating one metal with another

One metal can be coated with another by setting up electrodes and an electrolyte as shown in Figure 9.17.

The metal to be coated is the cathode and the metal to form the coating is made into the anode and is also present in the electrolyte. When the current of electricity is switched on, the metal from the anode dissolves in the electrolyte and metal in the electrolyte comes out of solution and forms a coating on the cathode.

This process is used to give objects made of a cheap metal a coating of a more expensive metal, to make them look more attractive. For example, it is used to coat cheap metals with gold to make jewellery or with silver to make EPNS (electroplated nickel silver) cutlery and ornaments (see page 123).

Electroplating is also used to cover steel with chromium. The chromium gives the steel an attractive shiny surface and also protects the steel from rusting (see page 89).

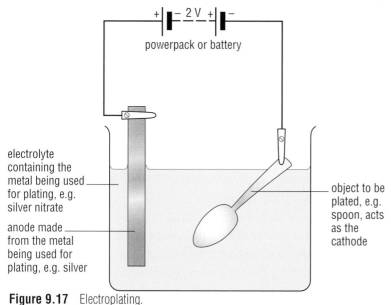

**Figure 9.17**   Electroplating.

electrolyte containing the metal being used for plating, e.g. silver nitrate

anode made from the metal being used for plating, e.g. silver

powerpack or battery

– 2 V

object to be plated, e.g. spoon, acts as the cathode

---

# ◆ SUMMARY ◆

◆ Metals and non-metals have different physical properties *(see page 104)*.
◆ Metal and non-metal oxides have different chemical properties *(see page 105)*.
◆ Some metals react with oxygen *(see page 105)*.
◆ Some metals react with water or steam *(see page 107)*.
◆ Some metals react with acids *(see page 109)*.
◆ A more reactive metal can displace a less reactive metal from a salt solution of the less reactive metal *(see page 109)*.
◆ Metals can be arranged in order of their reactivity in the reactivity series *(see page 110)*.
◆ Metals are used to generate electricity *(see page 111)*.
◆ Electricity can pass through some solids and liquids *(see page 114)*.
◆ Electrolysis can be used to separate elements *(see page 115)*.
◆ Electricity can be used to extract some metals *(see page 117)*.
◆ Electroplating is the coating of one metal with another using electricity *(see page 118)*.

---

## *End of chapter questions*

**1**   What is the reactivity series and how can it be used?
**2**   How can chemical processes be used to produce electricity?
**3**   How can electricity be used to separate materials?

# 10 *Earth materials*

Both metals and non-metals are extracted from the Earth and turned into useful products.

## Metals

Metals differ from each other in the way they react with other elements and compounds. Some metals, such as gold and silver, are very unreactive and can be found in their metallic form in the Earth's crust. Elements which are found on their own in this way are called native elements. More reactive metals are found combined with other elements. A rock which is rich in a metal compound is called an ore.

Different methods of extracting metals are used. They depend on the reactivity of the metal. For example, copper is quite unreactive and so can be extracted from its ore by roasting the ore in a furnace. Iron, which is more reactive, must be heated strongly in a blast furnace. This provides more heat energy which is needed for the reactions to release iron from its ore. Aluminium is more reactive than iron and needs even more energy to extract it. This energy is supplied by electricity.

In the sections that follow, the metals are arranged in order of their reactivity. The order starts with the least reactive and ends with aluminium – the most reactive of the metals we use in large amounts.

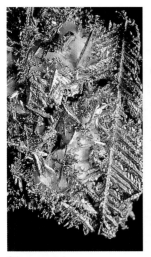  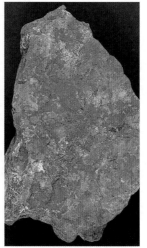 

Silver crystals    Gold crystals    Aluminium ore (bauxite)    Iron ore (haematite)

**Figure 10.1**  A selection of ores and native metals.

## *Alloys*

In the following descriptions of metals the word alloy will appear. Most metals in their pure form tend to be weak and soft. They are strengthened by mixing them with one or more other elements, usually different metals. These mixtures are called alloys. They are made by melting the metals, mixing them together and then allowing them to cool. The properties of an alloy can be changed by changing the proportions of the metals that are mixed together.

## Gold

Gold is found on its own as a metal. It forms in hydrothermal vents in the Earth's crust. These are spaces in the rock which contain water that has been heated by volcanic activity or hot rocks in the crust. When the rock bearing the gold is weathered, it is carried away in streams and rivers and the gold settles out with the rock particles where they are deposited.

### *Extraction*

On a small scale, gold is extracted by panning. A sediment from a stream is put in a shallow, wok-shaped pan with some water and the pan is swirled. The water lifts the lighter rocks to the edge of the pan where they escape and the heavier particles of gold collect at the bottom.

**Figure 10.2** Panning for gold.

On a large scale, the deposits are mined. The ore which contains the gold is crushed and made into a powder. It is treated with potassium cyanide, in which the gold dissolves. The solution is filtered from rocky parts of the ore and the gold is removed from the solution by a precipitation reaction (see page 66).

## Properties and uses

Gold does not react with the air and never loses its shine. It is soft and can be easily shaped or made into a thin sheet that does not break. The colour and shininess of gold make it an attractive material for jewellery. A very thin sheet of gold is called gold leaf and it is used for decoration of surfaces on buildings and books.

Gold is also used to make contacts that form the connections between wires in electrical circuits. This is because it does not corrode and this prevents the circuits from breaking.

The purity of gold is measured in carats. 24 carat gold is pure gold and 18 carat gold is 75% pure gold.

Gold is alloyed with other metals. White gold is an alloy of gold, nickel and palladium. Rolled gold is a thin layer of a gold alloy that is bonded onto brass or nickel silver.

**Figure 10.3**  Gold objects.

1  What is the purity of **a)** 22, **b)** 14 and **c)** 9 carat gold?
2  Why do you think gold is alloyed with less expensive metals?

# Silver

Silver may be found on its own as a metal. It forms in hydrothermal vents in the Earth's crust. A black mineral called silver glance which is formed from silver sulphide may also be found with the silver metal. Silver that has already been used is recycled. Coins containing silver and industrial wastes, particularly from the photographic industry, are sources of recycled silver.

## Extraction

Most silver extracted today is collected during the purification of copper, zinc and lead ores.

## *Properties and uses of silver*

Silver has the highest reflectivity of light of any metal. This means that its surface reflects more of the light shining onto it than the surface of other metals. This property makes it particularly attractive for use in jewellery, cutlery and ornaments. It is a soft metal in its pure form and is hardened by alloying it with copper to make sterling silver.

Electroplated nickel silver or EPNS is made from nickel silver (an alloy of copper and nickel) that is covered in a thin coating of silver.

Silver reacts with sulphur in the air to form a coating of silver sulphide, which is black, on the surface. This reduces the reflectivity of the metal and the silver is said to be tarnished.

**3** Why do you think sterling silver is better for cutlery than pure silver?

**Figure 10.4** Silver objects.

## Copper

The ore from which copper is extracted is called chalcopyrite or copper pyrites. It contains copper, iron and sulphur, is brass yellow, and is found in igneous and metamorphic rocks.

### *Extraction*

The ore is concentrated in a flotation cell (see Figure 3.8 page 38) and the copper, iron and sulphur are separated by roasting the ore in a furnace. The copper that is removed from the furnace still contains impurities. They are removed by making the copper into large slabs and hanging them in an electrical cell (see Figure 10.5). Each slab is an anode. As the electricity passes through the cell, the copper at the anode dissolves in the electrolyte and comes out of solution again on the cathode where it forms pure copper (see page 118). Gold and silver impurities in the metal fall to the bottom of the cell below the anode and form the anode sludge. They are removed and separated.

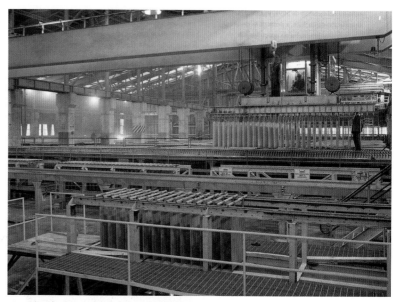

**Figure 10.5**   Making pure copper by electrolysis.

4 What are the three processes used in the extraction of copper?

5 What other metals are there in copper ore?

6 What properties of copper make it useful for electrical wiring in a home?

## *Properties and uses*

Copper is a soft metal that can be easily shaped. It does not react with water so it is used to make water pipes, though large water pipes are often made of plastic which is cheaper. It conducts heat well and is used in the bases of some kinds of kitchen pan. Copper's softness also allows it to be pulled out into a wire and as it also conducts electricity well and corrodes very slowly, the wire can be used to conduct electricity inside buildings.

Copper is alloyed with tin to make bronze. This alloy was first made and used 5000 years ago and its name is used to describe a period of history in which a great many bronze implements were used – the Bronze Age. Bronze is a particularly sonorous metal (it makes a ringing sound) and it is used to make bells and cymbals because of the clear ringing sound it produces when it is struck.

**Figure 10.6**   A 16th Century Benin bronze.

**7** Why is brass better for use in plug pins than copper?

Brass is an alloy of copper and zinc. It is strong, corrosion-resistant and is used to make the pins in electrical plugs. It is also a shiny metal and is used to make ornaments.

## Lead

Lead is extracted from a mineral called galena. This forms grey, crystal cubes and is a compound of lead and sulphur called lead sulphide. It is found in sedimentary rocks such as limestone.

### *Extraction*

**8** How does the extraction of lead compare with that of copper?

**9** How would you expect the weight of a piece of lead to compare with that of a piece of aluminium the same size? Explain your answer.

Lead ore is concentrated in a flotation cell (see Figure 3.8 page 38), then mixed with coke and heated in a blast furnace. The concentrated ore is roasted in air. Impure lead called bullion is produced. It contains copper and tin. These are removed by using a cell like the one used in the purification of copper (see Figure 10.5).

### *Properties and uses*

Lead is easily shaped and does not corrode. It can be used as flashing on roofs. This is a metal strip that is put over a place where a roof meets a wall on a building. The metal prevents water from going between the wall and the roof and leaking into the building. Lead can also be shaped to cover the edges of corrugated roofs. Lead is used in car batteries to generate electricity.

Lead is a metal with a very high density. This enables it to stop dangerous radiation from radioactive materials. Staff working in the X-ray departments of hospitals and in laboratories where radioactive materials are handled wear clothing containing lead to protect them.

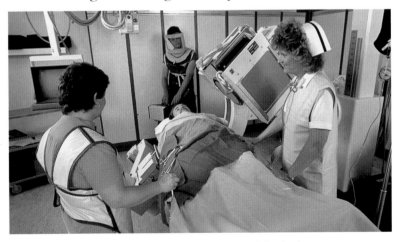

**Figure 10.7** X-ray staff wear protective clothes containing lead.

Lead and tin are mixed together to make alloys. One alloy is called solder and has a low melting point. It is used to connect wires in electrical circuits and to seal cans. A second alloy is called pewter. This can be easily shaped and is used to make ornaments and tankards for holding beer.

## Iron

The ore from which iron is extracted is called haematite (see Figure 10.1). It is found in igneous and sedimentary rocks in many parts of the world. Iron is combined with oxygen in haematite to form iron oxide.

### *Extraction*

Iron is separated from the oxygen in iron oxide by a reduction process. This takes place in a blast furnace (see Figure 10.8). The iron ore is mixed with coke and limestone and tipped into the top of the blast furnace. Hot air is blown into the blast furnace through pipes close to the base of the furnace.

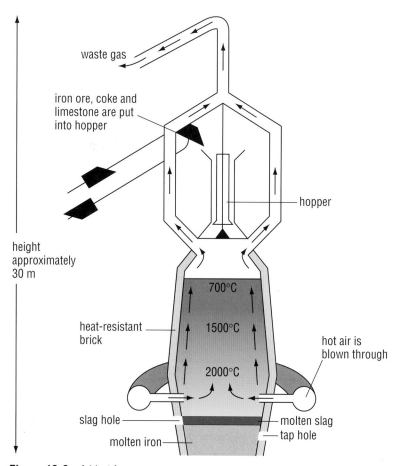

**Figure 10.8** A blast furnace.

10  Write word equations for the reactions which take place inside the blast furnace. Make a simple sketch of the furnace and indicate on it where each of the reactions takes place.

11  Why is limestone added to the ore and the coke?

12  How many tonnes of iron are produced in a blast furnace, if it produces 10 000 tonnes per day non-stop for 10 years?

13  How does using the gases from the top of the blast furnace to heat the incoming air make the iron cheaper to produce?

14  How do you think the blast furnace got its name?

The hot air causes the coke to ignite and burn strongly, raising the temperature as high as 2000°C. The carbon in the burning coke reacts with oxygen in the hot air to form carbon dioxide. This gas rises through the hot coke higher up the furnace and reacts with the carbon in it to form carbon monoxide. As the carbon monoxide rises in the furnace it reacts with the iron oxide in the ore to produce carbon dioxide and iron. The metal is in a solid form which has tiny holes in it.

As the iron sinks down the blast furnace it gets hotter and melts. The limestone also sinks with the iron and the heat causes the calcium carbonate from which it is made to break down into calcium oxide and carbon dioxide. The rocky substance in the iron ore is silicon oxide which does not melt at the high temperatures in the furnace. However the calcium oxide combines with the silicon oxide to make calcium silicate, which is known as slag. This substance melts in the high temperatures of the blast furnace and flows out with the molten iron. The slag floats on the molten iron and is easily separated from it.

## Pig iron

The iron which is drawn out of the bottom of the blast furnace is run down a channel which has a series of moulds branching from it on one side. This arrangement of channel and moulds is similar to the way piglets lie when they feed from their mother and the metal that flows into the channel and moulds is called pig iron.

# Early iron workers

Very rarely, iron occurs as a native metal. Some metal iron is formed where hot volcanic rock meets a seam of coal. The heat allows a chemical reaction to take place between the iron compounds in the rock and carbon in the coal. Many meteorites that strike the Earth are made of iron. It is possible that early people knew of metal iron but as the pieces were so rare they did not begin to make iron products on a large scale.

A chance heating of an iron ore in a charcoal fire most probably led to the discovery of the extraction of iron and the development of metal products. Before this discovery was made, bronze was the most common metal in everyday use. It is an alloy of copper and tin, but it is quite weak. Soldiers using bronze swords in battle had to stop occasionally to straighten them!

Iron is a stronger metal than bronze and soon replaced it as the most common metal for everyday uses.

*(continued)*

The Hittites were the first people to produce iron in large amounts about 3500 years ago. They were a people that lived in the land now called Turkey.

Iron needed a higher temperature than copper or tin for extraction from its ore. The extraction was achieved by heating the ore with charcoal and using bellows to supply more air to the furnace.

The iron made in these early furnaces was wrought iron. This is a soft form of iron. The Hittites discovered how to give the wrought iron a coating of harder metal by allowing the iron surface to combine with some of the carbon in the charcoal and form steel.

1 How do you think the discovery of iron affected warfare between countries?
2 What substance in the air takes part in a chemical reaction in the furnace?
3 How did the use of bellows help in the extraction of iron?
4 Steel is an alloy. From what substances is it made?
5 How did the discovery made by iron workers in Northern India differ from that made by the Hittites?

In Northern India, the iron workers developed a process which prevented wrought iron from rusting. In 400 BC they made a pillar of wrought iron 8 metres high and 6 tonnes in weight. This pillar is still standing today and does not have any rust (see Figure A). Nobody knows how these early iron workers made such a metal.

**Figure A** This wrought iron pillar was built in 400 BC and is still standing.

## Properties and uses of cast iron

When pig iron is re-melted it can be poured or cast into more complicated moulds and is known as cast iron. As the metal cools it expands a little and fills every part of the mould. This makes it suitable for use in complicated moulds like those used to make car engine blocks (see Figure 10.9). Cast iron is also strong and is used for manhole covers in the street since the metal can support the weight of traffic running over it. However, cast iron is brittle. This means that the metal breaks easily if it is bent, so it cannot be shaped by bending after it has cooled and set.

**Figure 10.9**   A cast iron engine block.

## *Steel*

The properties of pig and cast iron are due to the large amounts of carbon in the metal (up to 4%). This amount of carbon is reduced by placing the iron in a basic oxygen furnace with limestone and scrap metal and blasting a jet of oxygen into it from a water-cooled oxygen pipe.

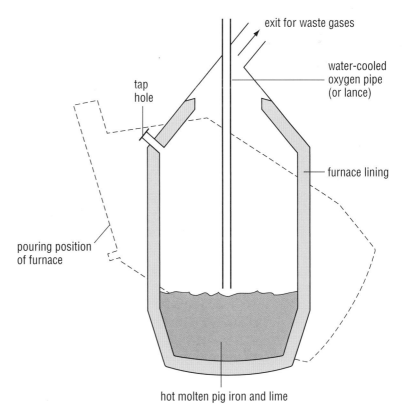

**Figure 10.10**   A basic oxygen furnace.

The oxygen combines with the carbon to form carbon dioxide and carbon monoxide. The amount of carbon left in the metal can be controlled and several types of steel can be made, each with a different amount of carbon from the others.

### Properties and uses of steel

Steel rusts, but if it is alloyed with nickel and chromium it forms stainless steel which does not rust. Stainless steel does not corrode in acidic conditions. This means that the metal does not wear away or break up so it is used in chemical plants where acids are used. Steel is used for making magnets but it can lose its magnetism in time. When steel is alloyed with cobalt, a magnetic metal is made which does not lose its magnetism. It is used for making permanent magnets.

## Zinc

The most common ore from which zinc is extracted is called zinc blende or sphalerite. It is found with the ores of lead and in limestone. It is made of the compound zinc sulphide.

## Extraction

Zinc ore is concentrated in the flotation cell (see Figure 3.8 page 38) then roasted in a furnace. Oxygen from the air combines with the zinc to form zinc oxide and with the sulphur to form sulphur dioxide. The zinc oxide is mixed with coke and heated in a blast furnace to 1400°C. The oxygen from the zinc oxide combines with the carbon from the coke to form carbon monoxide. Zinc has a boiling point of 908°C so in the blast furnace the metal vaporises as it forms. The zinc vapour is drawn out of the blast furnace and cooled.

## Uses of zinc

Zinc is used for the casing of cells in torches where it helps in the generation of electricity (see Figure 9.9 page 112). When zinc is exposed to the air it forms a layer of zinc oxide on its surface that prevents further corrosion of the metal. Like lead, it is used in flashing on roofs to prevent water penetrating the gap between chimney stacks and the roof tiles. Zinc is also used to coat steel in a process called galvanising. The galvanised steel is protected from rusting even if the zinc coating is broken.

**15** What would you expect to happen if cast iron was bent? Explain your answer.

**16** Why is the metal pipe in the oxygen furnace cooled with water?

**17** How can steel be made rust-proof?

**Figure 10.11** A galvanised steel crash barrier.

**18** How is the extraction of zinc in a blast furnace different from that of iron?

**19** Why is zinc a better metal to use for flashing than iron?

# Aluminium

The ore from which aluminium is extracted is called bauxite (see Figure 10.1). This rock is formed from a mixture of minerals that have been weathered in tropical regions of the world.

Aluminium was present as aluminium silicate when the rock first formed but the hot moist conditions removed the silicon and left behind a rock rich in aluminium hydroxide.

## *Extraction*

Bauxite is dug up from the surface of the Earth's crust and is broken into small pieces in a crushing machine. The pieces are mixed with sodium hydroxide solution and the mixture is heated under pressure in a large sealed tank. The aluminium oxide from the ore dissolves in the solution to form sodium aluminate. The solution is filtered to remove the other rocky substances and allowed to cool.

In the cooling process, crystals of aluminium oxide form which are separated from the solution of sodium hydroxide. The crystals are then heated and the water of crystallisation escapes from them – leaving aluminium oxide in powdered form.

Aluminium is extracted from aluminium oxide by electrolysis. This means that the aluminium oxide must be in liquid form for the elements to be separated. The melting point of aluminium oxide is high and a great deal of energy would be needed to melt it, so an alternative method that uses less energy is used. The aluminium oxide is dissolved in molten cryolite – a mineral formed from sodium aluminium fluoride. The electricity is passed through this mixture in a cell as shown in Figure 10.12.

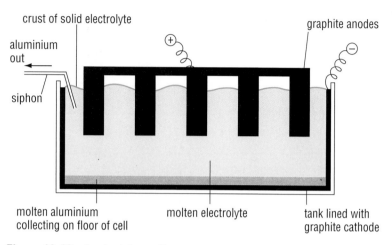

crust of solid electrolyte

aluminium out

siphon

graphite anodes

molten aluminium collecting on floor of cell

molten electrolyte

tank lined with graphite cathode

**Figure 10.12** An aluminium cell.

Before the development of electrolysis for the extraction of aluminium, it was so difficult to extract that it was prized more than gold and silver and was the most expensive metal. Today, it is widely used because it is cheap to produce using electricity from hydro-electric power stations.

## *Properties and uses*

Aluminium is soft, weak, light in weight and non-toxic. These properties make it useful for wrapping foods to keep them fresh. Aluminium is also a good conductor of electricity and, as it is light, these two properties make it useful for overhead power cables. Aluminium is also a good conductor of heat and, being lightweight, it is useful for making kitchen pans. The strength of aluminium is increased by mixing it with other metals. For example, aluminium is alloyed with copper to form a strong lightweight material for making aircraft and truck bodies and the frames for racing bicycles.

Aluminium is alloyed with copper and tin to make aluminium bronze. This is a strong, lightweight and corrosion-resistant metal which is used for fittings on the decks of boats and ships.

## Plastics and metals

There are many different kinds of plastic. Each one has properties which make it suitable for one or more uses. The properties of some plastics make them more suitable for a particular use than a metal. For example, in the past cast iron was used for gutters and down pipes on the outside of buildings to take away the rain water that fell on the roof. In time, the cast iron rusts. Today it has

**20** Why is the metal's lightness a particularly useful property?

**21** As the aluminium in the aluminium oxide collects at the cathode, what would you expect to collect at the anode?

been replaced by PVC (polyvinyl chloride) which does not rust. Iron was used to make baths. Today, most baths are made from acrylic plastics. Metals have also been used to make containers such as buckets, watering cans and waste bins. Although some metals are still used in this way, many containers are now made from polythene and polypropylene plastics.

# Non-metals

The non-metals carbon and sulphur are also extracted from the ground and have useful properties.

## Carbon

Most of the carbon in the Earth's crust is combined with other elements to make compounds called carbonates. Carbon also exists in pure forms which have different structures. These different forms are called allotropes. The three allotropes of carbon are graphite, diamond and buckminsterfullerene. Charcoal is an impure form of carbon which is a useful material.

### *Graphite*

Graphite is found in some igneous and metamorphic rocks. It is also made artificially by using electricity to heat coke for several hours to a temperature of about 2500°C. This way of producing graphite artificially is called the Archeson process.

The way the atoms of carbon join together to form graphite is shown in Figure 10.13. The carbon atoms form layers. In each layer the carbon atoms are held strongly together to form hexagonal structures. The layers are only held together by weak forces.

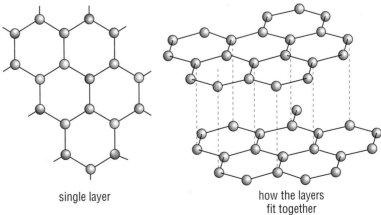

single layer       how the layers fit together

**Figure 10.13** The arrangement of carbon atoms in graphite.

### Properties and uses

Graphite is used to make the 'lead' in pencils. When a pencil point is drawn across the surface of paper the forces pulling on the graphite are stronger than the forces holding the layers together and the layers slide off each other onto the paper to make a pencil mark. Graphite in pencils is mixed with clay to give the 'lead' strength. The slipperiness of graphite also makes it a good lubricant to reduce the friction between the moving parts of machinery.

**22** Do you think a hard pencil has more clay or less clay than a soft pencil?

## *Diamond*

In the Earth's crust in Kimberley in South Africa there are pipes of rock. They have formed from molten rock rising up through the crust. The rock is called kimberlite and in some of the rock diamonds have formed. In other places diamonds have been found in the gravel in rivers and on beaches. They have been released from rock when the rock weathered.

Diamonds are made artificially by mixing carbon with nickel and squashing the mixture to 50 000 times atmospheric pressure and raising the temperature to 1500°C. After a few minutes very small diamonds are formed which can be used for industrial purposes.

The arrangement of carbon atoms in diamond is shown in Figure 10.14. The forces acting on each carbon atom are the same strength in each direction. This makes a very hard substance.

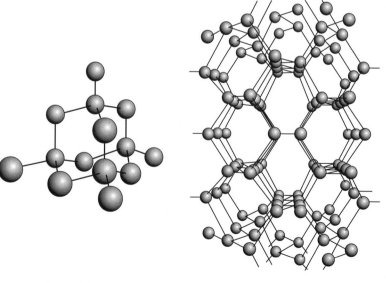

small part of the structure          larger part of the structure

**Figure 10.14**   Arrangement of carbon atoms in diamond.

### Properties and uses

Diamonds are used to drill through rock in search of oil and to cut through concrete, glass and metal. Most diamonds are dark and opaque but some are transparent. These diamonds are carefully cut to reflect the light and are highly prized for the way they sparkle. They are used to make jewellery.

## *Buckminsterfullerene*

This allotrope of carbon was discovered in 1985 and is named after the American architect, Buckminster Fuller, who built a domed roof over a sports stadium. There are 60 carbon atoms in a molecule of this allotrope and they are arranged like the material in the dome but they form a complete sphere called a 'bucky ball'.

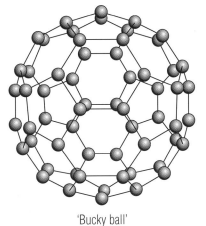

'Bucky ball'

**Figure 10.15** The 'bucky ball' has a similar structure to the dome at the Expo in Montreal, Canada.

## *Charcoal*

Wood charcoal is made by heating wood in the absence of air. In the past it was an important fuel and was used 3500 years ago to reduce iron oxide in iron ore to obtain iron metal. Charcoal absorbs smoke and this property makes it a suitable fuel for cooking food in barbecues.

Charcoal absorbs poisonous gases and is used in gas masks. It is used in aquarium filters to clean the water in fish tanks and in oven hoods to remove the smells of cooking in kitchens.

**23** Compare graphite and diamond.

**24** Carbon has a wide range of uses. Assess this statement with examples.

## *Coke*

Coke is made by heating coal without air. It is used to reduce the oxides of metals in the production of metals such as iron, zinc and lead.

## Sulphur

Sulphur is an element that escapes as a gas from the vent of a volcano. The solid sulphur forms a crust on rocks in the volcano vent. Large amounts of sulphur are also found in sedimentary rocks such as limestone. The sulphur moves into the sedimentary rocks from volcanic regions by melting and flowing through the crust over a long period of time.

### *Extraction*

Sulphur is sometimes extracted from natural gas but most of it is extracted from limestone rocks in the USA. The rocks are at least 100 metres below the surface and are covered in sand. Mining is not possible because mine shafts cannot be safely constructed in sand as the walls easily collapse. In addition, if the limestone rocks could be reached the smell of the sulphur would be unbearable and sulphur dioxide, a poisonous gas, would be produced as the rocks heated during drilling. In 1894, Herman Frasch (1851–1914) invented a sulphur pump to extract sulphur from the rocks (see Figure 10.16).

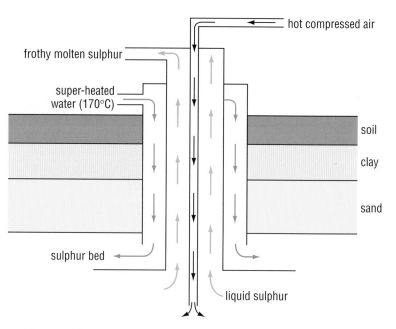

**Figure 10.16** The Frasch sulphur pump.

The pump works because sulphur has a melting point of 115°C and enough heat can be supplied to the rock by super-heated water to melt the sulphur and pump it out. Super-heated water is made by heating water under pressure until its temperature reaches 170°C.

There are three pipes arranged concentrically (one around the next) which connect the surface of the ground to the beds of sulphur in the rock. Super-heated water is pumped down the outer pipe and into the sulphur bed. Its heat transfers to the sulphur and melts it. Compressed air is pumped down the central pipe. Its pressure is 15 times that of the air and it pushes the mixture of molten sulphur and hot water up the middle pipe. The sulphur and water emerge from the pipe as a froth. This is poured into a vat where the water and sulphur cool. The water is drained off the solid sulphur. The sulphur is almost pure and can be used straight away for industrial purposes.

**25** Draw a cross section of the pipes used in the sulphur pump. State what each contains and the direction of its movement.

**Figure 10.17** Sticks of sulphur extracted by the Frasch process.

## *Properties*

Sulphur is a yellow solid at room temperature. It is brittle and does not dissolve in water. It burns in the air to form sulphur dioxide. This gas is used in the manufacture of sulphuric acid (see page 141).

Sulphur reacts with rubber when the two are heated together. It binds the long molecules of rubber together and stops them sliding past each other. Rubber treated with sulphur is called vulcanised rubber. It is much harder than natural rubber and tough enough for use in tyres on all kinds of cars and trucks.

Sulphur is poisonous to fungi and powdered sulphur is used as a fungicide.

# ◆ SUMMARY ◆

- ◆ A few metals are found uncombined with other elements in the Earth's crust, but most are present in compounds *(see page 120)*.
- ◆ Metals can be mixed to form alloys *(see page 121)*.
- ◆ Gold is used to make electrical contacts and for decorative purposes *(see page 122)*.
- ◆ Silver has properties that are useful for decorative purposes *(see page 123)*.
- ◆ Copper is purified by electrolysis *(see page 123)*.
- ◆ Lead is extracted by roasting the ore in air, then reducing lead oxide in a blast furnace *(see page 125)*.
- ◆ Iron is extracted from iron oxide by a reduction reaction in the blast furnace *(see page 126)*.
- ◆ Steel is produced from iron by reducing the amount of carbon in the iron *(see page 129)*.
- ◆ Zinc is extracted by roasting the ore in air to make zinc oxide which is then reduced in a blast furnace *(see page 130)*.
- ◆ Aluminium is extracted from aluminium oxide by electrolysis *(see page 131)*.
- ◆ There are three pure forms of carbon. They are graphite, diamond and buckminsterfullerene *(see page 133)*.
- ◆ Charcoal is a useful form of impure carbon *(see page 135)*.
- ◆ Sulphur is extracted using super-heated water and has a wide range of uses *(see page 136)*.

## *End of chapter question*

**1** Construct a table that summarises the information about the metals and non-metals in this chapter. Use headings such as sources, extraction and properties.

# 11 The chemical industry

Chemicals react together to make many of the materials around us. They are used to make the paper and inks in this book, the fibres and colours of your clothes, the walls and windows of the building around you, the contents of the rooms in the building, from cushions to computers, and the contents of your last meal. Some of these reactions happened naturally while others were controlled by people. Materials produced by the chemical industry are used in all forms of transport from bicycles to space craft and are used in farms and factories in the production of our food.

There can be many stages in the production of a material. At each stage, a process such as heating or cooling or a chemical reaction takes place. Often both a process and a reaction take place at the same time.

When the production of a new material is being worked out, the reactions and processes are carried out in the laboratory with laboratory apparatus. When the chemical engineers consider these reactions and processes to be working safely they design a chemical factory or plant to make the product (see Figure 11.1). The aim of the plant is to provide large amounts of the material cheaply, safely and without damaging the environment (see also Chapter 12).

1 List ten products that you think are made by the chemical industry.

**Figure 11.1** A chemical engineer initially works on plans using a computer.

2 Why must chemical engineers consider the price of the product they are making?

**Figure 11.2** Chemical engineers at work on building a new chemical plant.

## Women chemical engineers

Before the Industrial Revolution all products were made by the batch process. In this process the substances that are used to make a product are mixed, chemical reactions are allowed to take place and a certain amount of the product is made.

During and after the Industrial Revolution, larger amounts of products were needed more frequently. Chemists re-examined the ways some products were made and devised ways of making them by a continuous process. They worked at designing and building new, large pieces of equipment and at linking them together to form a chemical plant which could produce a product continuously. They also operated the chemical plants.

Chemists who took on work in improving the chemical industry became known as chemical engineers. At first, almost all chemical engineers were men but by 1990 a third of all new graduate chemical engineers were women.

Opportunities for women to develop careers in chemical engineering continue and some women now hold posts such as professorships and receive awards such as the Fellowship of the Institution of Chemical Engineers which were once only given to men.

**Figure A**  Rachel Spooncer is a fellow of the Institution of Chemical Engineers. She was elected to the UK Royal Academy of Engineering in 1996.

1 How does a continuous process compare with a batch process?
2 What type of work does a chemical engineer do?
3 How has the proportion of men and women working in chemical engineering changed over the years?

# Raw materials

A raw material is a substance that is used at the beginning of a process in the chemical industry to make new materials. For example, iron ore, limestone and coke are the raw materials from which iron is made (see page 126). Air is the raw material from which oxygen, nitrogen, argon and other gases are extracted (see page 79).

**Figure 11.3**  Limestone cliffs.

Water is used as a coolant and a solvent in chemical processes but it is also used as a raw material from which hydrogen is made. Salt (sodium chloride) is extracted from sea water.

The fossil fuels of coal, oil and gas are also used as raw materials and provide a wide range of chemical products. Coal, for example, provides creosote which is used in preserving wood and carbolic acid which is used in making some kinds of soap.

## Sulphuric acid

The raw materials for the manufacture of sulphuric acid are sulphur, oxygen and water. The manufacturing process takes place in three stages.

### 1 Production of sulphur dioxide

The raw materials for this stage are sulphur and oxygen. Sulphur is heated until it melts and it is then sprayed into a furnace containing dry air. The following reaction takes place:

$$sulphur + oxygen \rightarrow sulphur\ dioxide$$

### 2 Production of sulphur trioxide

Sulphur dioxide combines with more oxygen to form sulphur trioxide:

$$sulphur\ dioxide + oxygen \rightleftharpoons sulphur\ trioxide$$

The reaction is slow at room temperature and at very high temperatures the reaction is reversible (see page 57). The process used to speed up this reaction is called the Contact process. The gases are heated to 400–500°C. Their pressure is increased to twice that of the atmosphere, then they are passed over trays of the catalyst vanadium oxide.

**3** How is sulphur made to react with oxygen?

**4** Why do you think the pressure of the gases was increased in stage 2?

**5** How did the catalyst help the reaction? (See page 67 to help you answer.)

**6** In which stage are the processes of dissolving and diluting carried out? Explain your answers.

### 3 Production of sulphuric acid

The sulphur trioxide dissolves in sulphuric acid and forms a liquid called oleum. The reaction is:

$$sulphur\ trioxide + sulphuric\ acid \rightarrow oleum$$

Sulphuric acid is made by diluting the oleum with water. The reaction is:

$$oleum + water \rightarrow sulphuric\ acid$$

## Uses of sulphuric acid

**Figure 11.4** A tin of vegetable soup.

The ways in which sulphuric acid affects our lives may be considered in more detail by taking an everyday object such as a can of vegetable soup. The plants which form the soup were grown with the aid of fertilisers. Sulphuric acid is used to make a type of fertiliser called ammonium sulphate and it is also used to make calcium sulphate – a component of a fertiliser called superphosphate.

The vegetables have been processed in a factory where detergents are used to clean the working surfaces and utensils used to make the soup. Detergents are made from reactions which take place between sulphuric acid and chemicals extracted from oil (see page 145).

The can of soup may have been delivered to the shop or supermarket in a white van. The colour is due to titanium, a metal extracted from its ore by using sulphuric acid. The lights and other electrical components on the van are powered from the battery which contains sulphuric acid.

**For discussion**

How could the facts that sulphuric acid is used in the making of fibres, soap and insecticide be used in the story of the can of soup?

# Sodium hydroxide

## Manufacture of sodium hydroxide

Sodium hydroxide is made by the electrolysis of a solution of sodium chloride called brine. Chlorine and hydrogen are also produced.

## Uses of sodium hydroxide

Sodium hydroxide is used for making a wide variety of chemicals, synthetic fibres, soap, oven cleaners, bleach, dyes and pharmaceuticals. It is also used in the extraction of aluminium (see page 132) and in the processing of wood to make paper.

**7** What is the raw material from which sodium hydroxide is made?

**8** How does sodium hydroxide help to keep your home clean?

**9** How has sodium hydroxide helped in the production of this book?

**10** How does a rocket entering space depend on brine?

## *Uses of chlorine and hydrogen*

The uses of chlorine and hydrogen are shown in Figure 11.5. Hydrogen is used in the making of margarine – it reacts with vegetable oils and turns them from liquids into solids. It is also used in rocket fuel and in the manufacture of plastics from oil products (see page 132).

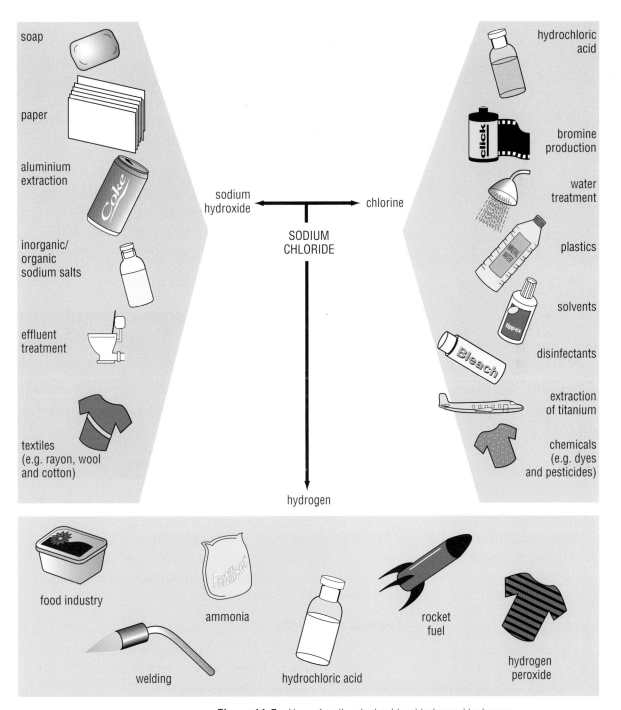

soap

paper

aluminium extraction

sodium hydroxide ⟷ chlorine

SODIUM CHLORIDE

inorganic/ organic sodium salts

effluent treatment

textiles (e.g. rayon, wool and cotton)

hydrochloric acid

bromine production

water treatment

plastics

solvents

disinfectants

extraction of titanium

chemicals (e.g. dyes and pesticides)

hydrogen

food industry

ammonia

welding

hydrochloric acid

rocket fuel

hydrogen peroxide

**Figure 11.5** Uses of sodium hydroxide, chlorine and hydrogen.

# Ammonia

## *Manufacture of ammonia*

Ammonia is made from nitrogen in the air and hydrogen from natural gas. The reaction in which the two elements take part is a reversible one:

$$\text{nitrogen} + \text{hydrogen} \rightleftharpoons \text{ammonia}$$

Nitrogen is an unreactive gas, but Fritz Haber (1868–1934) devised a way of making it react with hydrogen to produce ammonia. The way the reaction was carried out is known as the Haber process. The original laboratory apparatus that Haber used was made out of carbon steel. This metal reacted with the hydrogen and slowly became brittle. The high temperatures and pressures under which the reaction was made to work caused the brittle metal to break. Karl Bosch (1874–1940) performed the engineering task of scaling up Haber's apparatus into an industrial plant. He replaced the carbon steel with a steel alloy that did not react with hydrogen. The ammonia plants designed by Bosch have a tall tower connected to a complicated arrangement of pipes, as in Figure 11.6.

**Figure 11.6** An ammonia plant.

**11** What are the raw materials from which ammonia is made?

**12** How important was Bosch's decision to change the metal used in the plant? Explain your answer.

**13** Why is the pressure of the gas mixture increased?

**14** In the production of what important product is ammonia used?

The mixture of pure nitrogen and hydrogen is heated to 450°C and its pressure is increased to over 250 times the pressure of the atmosphere. This helps to make sure that more ammonia is produced than is changed back into hydrogen and nitrogen.

### Uses of ammonia

Most of the ammonia that is produced is made into fertiliser to improve the growth of crops. Ammonia is also used to make oven cleaners and its chloride salt is used in dry cells (see page 112). Some ammonia is made into nitric acid (see opposite).

## Nitric acid

**15** What are the raw materials of nitric acid?

**16** How does nitric acid help in the blasting of rock out of the ground in a quarry?

Nitric acid is made by mixing ammonia with air. The process takes place in several stages during which the mixture of gases is heated to 900°C and passed over a catalyst made from platinum and rhodium.

Nitric acid is used to make fertiliser, explosives such as trinitrotoluene (TNT), pharmaceuticals and synthetic fibres.

# The petrochemical industry

Petrochemicals are made from petroleum and natural gas. Petroleum means rock oil. It is usually simply called oil.

Natural gas and oil are made from the dead bodies of tiny animals and plants that lived in the seas over 200 million years ago. The bodies decayed to form molecules called hydrocarbons. These are made of atoms of carbon and hydrogen as Figure 11.7 shows.

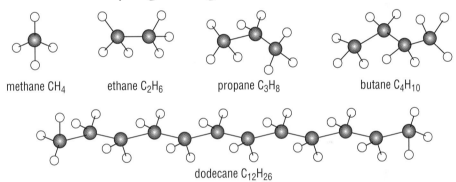

methane $CH_4$    ethane $C_2H_6$    propane $C_3H_8$    butane $C_4H_{10}$

dodecane $C_{12}H_{26}$

**Figure 11.7** Hydrocarbon structures.

The different hydrocarbons have different boiling points and fractional distillation is used to separate them.

## Fractional distillation of oil

### 1 Heating the oil

The oil is heated to about 450°C and most of it turns into a vapour. This is introduced into the fractional distillation column which forms a tall tower, as Figure 11.8 shows.

### 2 Separating the hydrocarbons

The bottom of the tower is kept at 360°C and the top of the tower is kept at 40°C. The hot oil vapour is introduced into the tower below the mid-way point. Inside the tower are tiers of trays (see Figure 11.9). There are tubes called risers passing through each tray. Above each riser is a bubble cap.

**Figure 11.8** Distillation towers.

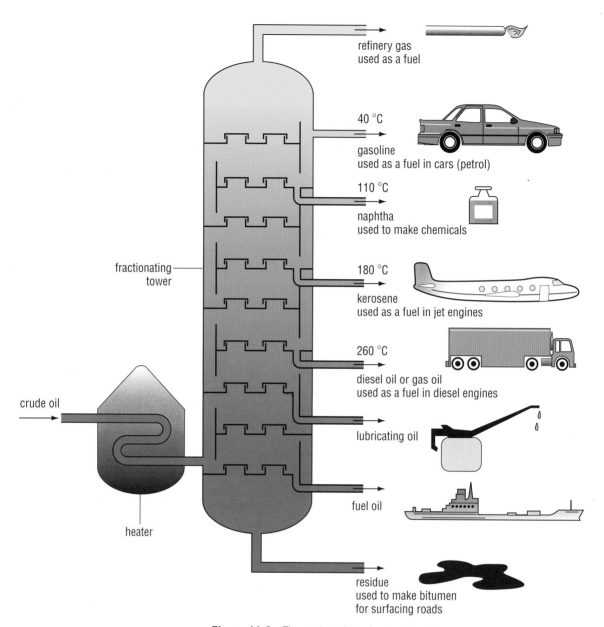

**Figure 11.9** The products from the fractions in the tower.

When the vapour meets a tray, some of it condenses and forms a liquid. When the tray is full, some of the liquid spills down the overflow into the tray below. The hydrocarbons in the vapour that did not condense pass upwards through the risers and out under the bubble cap onto the tray above. This tray is slightly cooler than the one below and some of the hydrocarbons condense and form a liquid. When hydrocarbons condense they give out heat energy into the liquid they enter. This heat causes other hydrocarbons in the mixture with lower boiling points to evaporate and rise into the tray above.

The fractional distillation of oil is a continuous process and a fully operational tower has liquids in every tray. Gases bubble through them from the trays below while liquids containing hydrocarbons with the longest molecules move downwards through the overflow pipes. There are collection pipes at different heights up the tower. They collect different fractions of the oil. Each fraction is a mixture of hydrocarbons with similar boiling points and they are used to make up a range of products, as Figure 11.9 shows.

**Table 11.1** The boiling points and range of carbon atoms in different oil fractions (simplified).

| Fraction of oil | Boiling points of liquids °C | Carbon atoms |
|---|---|---|
| A | 180 | 9–16 |
| B | 40 | 4–12 |
| C | 260 | 15–19 |
| D | below 40 | 1–4 |
| E | 110 | 7–14 |

## Cracking

There is a greater need for hydrocarbons with short chain molecules than for hydrocarbons with long chain molecules. Some of the oil from the fractionating column is heated and passed over a catalyst made from alumina – silica gel in powdered form.

The long chain hydrocarbons in the oil are cracked. This means that they are broken up into smaller chain molecules. These are then removed and separated by more fractional distillation equipment.

17 Table 11.1 shows the boiling points and range of carbon atoms in the molecules of five fractions of oil.

a) Arrange the letters of the fractions in order, starting with the one that would be drawn from the top of the tower.

b) Look at Figure 11.9, to identify the fractions and write down the products made from each one.

c) What is the relationship between the boiling points of the fractions and the lengths of the hydrocarbons they contain?

18 How do gases move up the tower?

19 How do liquids move down the tower?

20 Which fractions are used for transport?

21 Why is the cracking process used ?

# Finding a site for an industrial plant

A variety of raw materials may be used to make a product. They are found at different places in the world and have to be brought together. An industrial plant may be set up at, or near, the place where one or more raw materials are found and other raw materials are transported to the site. If large amounts of a raw material are to be transported, the cheapest and safest means of transport will be used. In many cases this form of transport is by ship. Other considerations to be taken into account when siting an industrial plant are the availability of water as it is needed for many stages of production and the availability of people to work in the plant.

Figure 11.10 shows a map of an area where two raw materials are found. The third raw material needed will have to be transported to the area by ship. After the product has been made, it will be transported to an area which is not on the map but to the south of it. This area can receive the product from other areas which are also not on the map. Money is available for setting up roads and railways in addition to setting up the plant and a docking area.

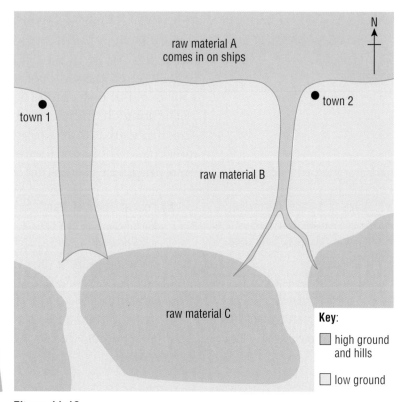

Figure 11.10

For discussion

Where should the industrial plant be built? Give reasons for your answer.

What issues were raised in coming to your decision?

# ◆ SUMMARY ◆

◆ The chemical industry provides us with many products *(see page 139)*.

◆ Chemical engineers scale up laboratory experiments into industrial plants *(see page 139)*.

◆ Sulphuric acid is made by the Contact process *(see page 141)*.

◆ Sodium hydroxide is made by electrolysis *(see page 142)*.

◆ Ammonia is made by the Haber process *(see page 144)*.

◆ Fractional distillation is used to separate the molecules in petrochemicals *(see page 145)*.

## End of chapter question

**1** What are the processes used in industry to convert raw materials into useful products?

# 12 Chemicals and the environment

The first people used natural materials such as stone, wood, animal skins, bones, antlers and shells. They shaped materials using flint knives and axes. When they discovered fire they also discovered the changes that heat could make.

First they saw how it changed food and later it is believed that they saw how metal was produced from hot rocks around a camp fire. In time, they learned how to extract metals from rocks by smelting and to use the metals to make a range of products (see Figure 12.1).

**Figure 12.1** A Bronze Age village scene.

The human population was only small when metal smelting was discovered and the smoke and smell from this process caused little pollution. As the human population grew, the demand for metal and other products such as pottery and glass increased. All the processing in the manufacture of these products had to be done by hand. Although there would be some pollution around the places where people gathered to make these products, the world environment was not threatened.

About 200 years ago it was discovered how machines could be used in manufacturing processes and the Industrial Revolution began. Machines could be used to produce more products than would be produced by people working on their own.

This meant that large amounts of fuel were needed to work the machines and air pollution increased (see Figure 12.2). Larger amounts of raw materials were needed and more habitats were destroyed in order to obtain them. More waste products were produced, increasing water and land pollution as the industrial manufacturing processes developed. The world population also increased, causing an increased demand for more materials which in turn led to more pollution and habitat destruction.

**Figure 12.2**   The smoky skyline of Glasgow in the mid 19th Century.

**1** What were the first materials people used?

**2** Why did the pollution caused by manufacturing materials not cause a serious threat to the environment until the Industrial Revolution?

**3** Why did people believe it was safe to release wastes into the environment?

At first, and for many years, it was believed that the air could carry away the fumes and make them harmless and that chemicals could be flushed into rivers and the sea where they would be diluted and become harmless. Also, the ways various chemical wastes could affect people were unknown.

An awareness of the dangers of pollution increased in the latter half of the 20th Century and in many countries today, steps are being taken to control it and develop more efficient ways of manufacturing materials.

*For discussion*

Some people believe that we must go back to the lifestyles of our earlier ancestors if the planet is to be saved. How realistic is this idea? Explain your answer.

## The Earth's changing atmosphere

Studies from astronomy and geology have shown that the Solar System formed from a huge cloud of gas and dust in space. The Earth is one of the planets formed from this cloud. The surface of the Earth was punctured with erupting volcanoes for a billion years after it formed. The gases escaping from inside the Earth through the volcanoes formed the first atmosphere. This was composed of carbon dioxide, water vapour, ammonia and methane.

**Figure A** A smoking volcano in Indonesia.

Three billion years ago the first plants developed. They produced oxygen as a waste product of photosynthesis.

As the plants began to flourish in both sea and fresh water and on the land, the amount of oxygen in the atmosphere increased. It reacted with ammonia to produce nitrogen.

**Figure B** Some early land plants were probably similar to modern day ferns.

*(continued)*

Bacteria developed which survived by using energy from the breakdown of nitrates in the soil. In this process more nitrogen was produced. In time, nitrogen and oxygen became the two major gases of the atmosphere. Between 15 and 30 kilometres above the Earth, the ultraviolet rays of the Sun reacted with oxygen to produce ozone. An ozone molecule is formed from three oxygen atoms. It prevents ultraviolet radiation, which is harmful to life, reaching the Earth's surface. If the ozone layer had not developed, life might not have evolved to cover such large areas of the planet's surface as it does today.

Today, owing to the activities of humans, the atmosphere contains increasing amounts of carbon dioxide, large amounts of sulphur dioxide and chlorofluorocarbons (CFCs) which have destroyed large portions of the ozone layer.

1 How has the composition of the atmosphere changed since the Earth first formed?

2 What has changed the composition of the atmosphere?

3 The atmospheres of Venus and Mars are like the atmosphere of the Earth in the first million years of its history. What can you infer from this information?

For discussion
How is the change in the ozone layer affecting people today?

For discussion
How would our lives change if power stations could no longer supply us with electricity?

# Air pollution

We burn large amounts of fuel, such as coal and oil, every day in power stations to produce electricity. This provides us with light, warmth and power. The power is used in all kinds of industries for the manufacture of a wide range of things, from clothes to cars. In the home, electricity runs washing machines, fridges and microwave ovens. It provides power for televisions, radios and computers. When coal and oil are burned, however, they produce carbon dioxide, carbon monoxide, sulphur dioxide, oxides of nitrogen and soot particles that make smoke.

**Figure 12.3** Electricity makes our lives more comfortable.

## Carbon dioxide

Carbon dioxide is described as a greenhouse gas because the carbon dioxide in the atmosphere acts like the glass in a greenhouse. It allows heat energy from the Sun to pass through it to the Earth, but prevents much of the heat energy radiating from the Earth's surface from passing out into space. The heat energy remains in the atmosphere and warms it up. The warmth of the Earth has allowed millions of different life forms to develop and it keeps the planet habitable.

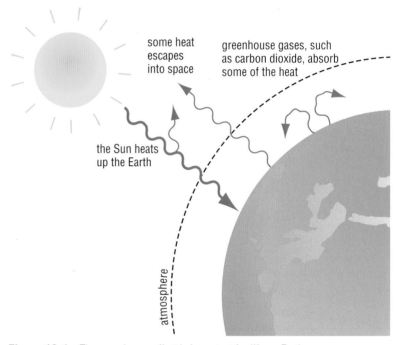

some heat escapes into space

greenhouse gases, such as carbon dioxide, absorb some of the heat

the Sun heats up the Earth

atmosphere

**Figure 12.4**  The greenhouse effect is important for life on Earth.

In the past the level of carbon dioxide in the atmosphere has remained low but now the level is beginning to rise. The extra carbon dioxide will probably trap more heat energy in the atmosphere. A rise in the temperature of the atmosphere will melt the ice at the Earth's poles. This will lead to a raising of the sea level and a change in the climate for almost all parts of the Earth. The rise in temperature is known as global warming.

## Carbon monoxide

Carbon monoxide is a very poisonous gas. It readily combines with the red pigment haemoglobin in the blood. Haemoglobin carries oxygen round the body but if carbon monoxide is inhaled, it combines with the haemoglobin and stops the oxygen being transported.

## Acid rain makers

Sulphur dioxide is produced by the combustion of sulphur in a fuel when the fuel is burned. Sulphur dioxide reacts with water vapour and oxygen in the air to form sulphuric acid. This may fall to the ground as acid rain or snow.

Oxides of nitrogen are converted to nitric acid in the atmosphere and this falls to the ground as acid rain or as snow.

### *Acid rain*

When acid rain reaches the ground it drains into the soil, dissolves some of the minerals there and carries them away. This process is called leaching. Some of the minerals are needed for the healthy growth of plants. Without the minerals the plants become stunted and may die (see Figure 12.5).

**Figure 12.5** Spruce trees in Bulgaria damaged by acid rain.

The acid rain drains into rivers and lakes and lowers the pH of the water. Many forms of water life are sensitive to the pH of the water and cannot survive if it is too acidic. If the pH changes, they die and the animals that fed on them, such as fish, may also die.

Acid rain leaches aluminium ions out of the soil. If they reach a high concentration in the water the gills of fish are affected. It causes the fish to suffocate.

# Soot and smog

**Figure 12.6** The London smog of 1952.

4 What property of soot particles affects photosynthesis?

5 Why is carbon monoxide a deadly gas?

6 A lake is situated near a factory that burns coal. How may the lake be affected in years to come if

a) there is no smoke control at the factory,

b) there is no smoke control world wide?

Explain your answers.

The soot particles in the air from smoke settle on buildings and plant life. They make buildings dirty and form black coatings on their outer surfaces. When soot covers leaves, it cuts down the amount of light reaching the leaf cells and slows down photosynthesis.

As well as being used in industry, coal used to be the main fuel for heating homes in the United Kingdom until the 1950s. In foggy weather the smoke from the coal combined with water droplets in the fog to form smog. The water droplets absorbed the soot particles and chemicals in the smoke and made a very dense cloud at ground level, through which it was difficult to see.

When people inhaled air containing smog the linings of their respiratory systems became damaged. People with respiratory diseases were particularly vulnerable to smog and in the winter of 1952, 5000 people died in London. This tragedy lead to the passing of laws to help reduce air pollution.

In Los Angeles, weather conditions in May to October lead to the exhaust gases from vehicles and smoke from industrial plants collecting above the city in a brown haze. Sunlight shining through this smog causes photochemical reactions to occur in it. This produces a range of chemicals including peroxyacetyl nitrate (PAN) and ozone. Both these chemicals are harmful to plants and ozone can produce asthma attacks in the people in the city below.

# The danger of lead

A combustion reaction takes place inside car engines. In this reaction, petrol is burned to release energy to push the pistons in the engine. In the past, lead was added to all petrol to improve the combustion reaction and the engine's performance. The exhaust gases carried the lead away as tiny particles. They were inhaled by people and settled on their food and skin. Lead in high

**7** In the Arctic regions, snow lies on the ground all winter. As spring approaches and the air warms up, some of the water in the snow evaporates. Later, all the snow melts.

**a)** How does the evaporation of the water in the snow affect the concentrations of acids in the snow?

**b)** Table 12.1 shows how the pH of a river in the Arctic may change during the spring.

| Week | pH |
|------|-----|
| 1 | 7.1 |
| 2 | 7.0 |
| 3 | 6.9 |
| 4 | 6.8 |
| 5 | 5.5 |
| 6 | 5.0 |
| 7 | 4.7 |
| 8 | 5.1 |
| 9 | 5.5 |
| 10 | 5.9 |

**i)** Plot a graph of the data.

**ii)** Why do you think the pH changed in weeks 5–7?

**iii)** Why do you think the pH changed in weeks 8–10?

**iv)** How do you expect the pH to change in the next few weeks after week 10? Explain your answer.

**8** Does a tall chimney solve the problem of air pollution? Explain your answer.

concentrations in the body causes damage to the nervous system including the brain. Children absorb lead into their bodies more readily than adults and in areas of cities where there are large amounts of exhaust gases from cars, high levels of lead have been found in children's blood.

# Improving air quality

The air around a factory can be kept clean by using a tall chimney to release the smoke high into the air (see Figure 12.7). Winds take the smoke away from the factory and its surrounding area. The harmful constituents in factory smoke can be removed chemically and physically.

**Figure 12.7** A factory with a very tall chimney.

## *Chemical removal of sulphur dioxide*

Sulphur dioxide can be removed in two ways to form useful products.

Lime can be sprayed into the waste gases where it combines with sulphur dioxide to form calcium sulphate. This rocky material can be used in making the foundation layer of roads.

**9** Treating waste gases is expensive. Calcium sulphate can be used as a building material in road making and ammonium sulphate can be used as a fertiliser.

**a)** How might treating waste gases affect the price of the product being made?

**b)** How might a company earn extra money after it has fitted equipment to treat waste gases? How will this affect the price of the product?

Ammonia can be mixed with waste gases where it reacts with sulphur dioxide to form ammonium sulphate, which can be used as a fertiliser.

## *Physical removal of particles*

Most of the particles in smoke have a small charge of static electricity. The particles can be removed by a device called an electrostatic precipitator. This device has highly charged metal plates. When the smoke passes through the precipitator, the particles are attracted to the plates and the remaining gases pass on.

## *Smokeless fuel*

Substances which cause harmful smoke can be removed from fuel before it is used. Coal, for example, can be heated without air to remove the tars and gas which make the coal burn with a smoky flame. Coal treated in this way forms the fuel called coke.

## *Unleaded petrol*

Engines have been developed which run on unleaded petrol, yet still give good performance.

## *Catalytic converters*

Many cars are now fitted with a catalytic converter. This device forms part of the exhaust system. Inside the converter is a catalyst made of platinum and rhodium. The waste gases from the engine take part in chemical reactions in the converter which produce water, nitrogen and carbon dioxide.

**10** The middle of a catalytic converter has a honeycomb structure. Why is this structure used?

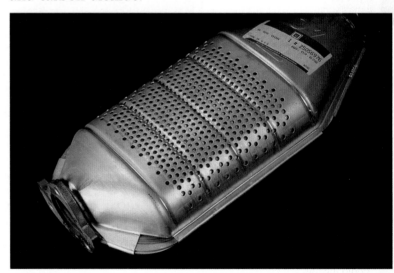

**Figure 12.8**   A catalytic converter.

## CFC replacements

CFCs have been replaced by carbon dioxide and hydrocarbon gases in the manufacture of aerosols and refrigerators in many countries.

For discussion

**What can we do to reduce air pollution?**

# Water pollution

## Fresh water

Fresh water, such as streams and rivers, has been used from the earliest times to flush away wastes. Over the last few centuries many rivers of the world have been polluted by a wide range of industries including textile and paper making plants, tanneries and metal works. People in many countries have become aware of the dangers of pollution and laws have been made to reduce it. Ways have been found to prevent pollution occurring and to recycle some of the materials in the wastes.

**Figure 12.9** This cellulose factory is causing the water to become polluted.

11 How are the lives of people who live by polluted rivers and catch fish from them put at risk?

12 The water flowing through a village had such low levels of mercury in it that it was considered safe to drink. Many of the villagers showed signs of mercury poisoning. How could this be?

The most harmful pollutants in water are the PCBs (polychlorinated biphenyls) and heavy metals such as cadmium, chromium, nickel and lead. In large concentrations these metals damage many of the organs of the body and can cause cancers to develop. PCBs are used in making plastics and, along with mercury compounds, are taken in by living organisms at the beginning of food chains (see *Biology Now! 11–14* pages 182–186). They are passed up the food chain as each organism is eaten by the next one along the chain. This leads to organisms at the end of the food chain having large amounts of toxic chemicals in their bodies which can cause permanent damage or death.

**Figure 12.10**  The excessive use of fertilisers leads to algal bloom in rivers and kills fish.

The careless use of fertilisers allows them to drain from the land into the rivers and lakes and leads to the overgrowth of water plants. When these die, large numbers of bacteria decompose the plants and as they do so, the bacteria take in oxygen from the water. The reduction in oxygen levels in the water kills many water animals. Phosphates in detergents also cause an overgrowth in water plants which can lead to the death of water animals in the same way.

## Sea water

The pollutants of fresh water are washed into the sea where they may collect in the coastal marine life. The pollutants may cause damage to the plants and animals that live in the sea and make them unfit to be collected for human food.

Large amounts of oil are transported by tankers across the ocean every day. In the past the tanker crew flushed out the empty oil containers with sea water to clean them. The oil that was released from the ship formed a film on the water surface which prevented oxygen entering the water from the air. It also reduced the amount of light that could pass through the upper waters of the sea to reach the phytoplankton and allow them to photosynthesise.

The problem of this form of oil pollution has been reduced by adopting a 'load on top' process, where the water used to clean out the containers is allowed to settle and the oil that has been collected floats to the top. This oil is kept in the tanker and is added to the next consignment of oil that is transported.

Occasionally a tanker is wrecked. When this happens large amounts of oil may spill out onto the water and be washed up onto the shore. This causes catastrophic damage to the habitat and even with the use of detergents and the physical removal of the oil the habitat may take years to recover.

**13**  How does oil floating on the surface of the sea affect the organisms living under it?

**Figure 12.11** Oil spills like this can have a huge effect on the sea and coastal wildlife.

# Chemicals and the land environment

The major chemical pollutants on land are pesticides which can affect human health and radioactive chemicals accidentally released from nuclear power plants which can cause cancer to develop. DDT is a pesticide that causes serious long term problems and it is now banned in many countries. However, it is still used in some countries where no laws exist to restrict its use. They continue to use it because it is very effective in controlling the mosquitoes that spread malaria.

The discarded products of manufacturing industries produce a pollution problem in every country. The tips in which the waste is stored take up space.

Today, many tips are carefully filled so that when they are full they can be covered with soil and new habitats established on top of them. While the rubbish is settling and decomposing on the tip some of it gives off methane gas. This can be collected by a system of pipes and used as a fuel.

**Figure 12.12**   A tip with a methane 'breather'.

Most raw materials have to be taken out of the ground. In some cases mine shafts are sunk into the ground and the material is removed with little damage to the surrounding habitat. Lead, zinc and some copper and coal are mined in this way.

In open cast mining, the land surface is removed to extract the raw material (see Figure 12.13). Aluminium and some coal and copper are removed like this. It causes complete habitat destruction. If this occurs in rainforest areas the forest may not be able to grow back again when the mining operation is over because the thin layer of soil on which the forest grew may have been completely washed away.

**14** How do the methods of extracting raw materials affect plants and animals that live in the same area?

**Figure 12.13**   Open cast mining in a rainforest in South America.

# Renewable and non-renewable materials

Raw materials can be divided into two groups – renewable materials and non-renewable materials. Wood is an example of a renewable material. As trees are cut down to provide the raw material for wood products, young trees are planted to replace them. Iron is an example of a non-renewable material. There is a certain amount of it in the Earth's crust which is not replaced after it is used up. As the iron ore is mined the supply left in the ground is reduced. In time there could be none left to use.

As the human population increases the demand for raw materials also increases. Although renewable materials can be replaced, the extra demand means that extra space has to be found for the material to be re-formed. This can result in habitat destruction. An example of this is where moorlands are planted with forests of fast growing trees to be used in manufacturing.

**Figure 12.14**  A coniferous forest being replanted.

As non-renewable raw materials cannot be replaced, studies have been made to find out how much of each material is left on the Earth. The rate at which the material is, at present, being used up is also calculated. If the figure for the world stock of a material is divided by the annual rate at which the material is being used up, we can find out how long the stock of the material will last. For example, iron ore stocks will probably only last until about the year 2300 but world stocks of copper ore may only last until about 2030.

**15** Many natural forests have a mixture of many different species of tree. They are of different ages and are irregularly spaced out. Many planted forests have very few tree species. The trees are the same age and are regularly spaced out.

**a)** In what ways are the planted forests different from the natural forests?

**b)** Do you think the two forests will support the same wildlife? Explain your answer.

**16** If the world stock of a material is 10 000 000 tonnes and it is used at a rate of 250 000 tonnes a year:

**a)** how long will the stocks last,

**b)** when will the stocks run out?

# Recycling

The products into which materials are made are often used only for a certain length of time. A newspaper may be read for a day, a bottle of lemonade may last three days, an item of clothing may last a year and a car may last 15 years. If the products are thrown away when their use is over the materials in them just stay in the ground in a tip. They take up space and have to be replaced by extracting more raw materials and using large amounts of energy in the manufacturing processes. Recycling the materials saves space, raw materials and energy.

Paper is made from smashing wood into a pulp of tiny fibres then binding them together in a thin sheet. When paper is recycled it is made into a pulp of fibres again, without having to use energy and chemicals to break down the wood.

Glass is made from sand, limestone and soda and a large amount of heat energy is required. Less energy is needed to melt recycled glass and make it ready for use again. The recycled glass is mixed with the raw ingredients as new glass products are made.

Large amounts of energy are needed for the extraction of metals such as iron (see page 126) and aluminium (see page 131). Less energy is needed to melt them down than to extract new metals from their ores. By recycling metals, less fuel is used and the stocks of the ores are conserved.

## Methods of separation

Materials for recycling can be separated by people and taken to recycling centres (see Figure 12.15) or they can be separated after the collection of refuse. The magnetic separator (see Figure 3.7 page 38) is used to separate iron and steel from other materials.

In industry, products which are wastes in one process can be collected and used elsewhere. For example, in the purification of copper the metals silver and gold are produced (see page 123). These metals are not discarded but sold to people such as jewellery manufacturers who can use them.

Some of the reactions which take place in the chemical industry produce heat energy. This is not released but used in other parts of the chemical plant. For example, the heat produced when sulphur and oxygen combine in a combustion reaction is used to melt the solid sulphur at the beginning of the process to manufacture sulphuric acid.

17 Imagine that a new product had been invented that uses the material in question 16. An extra 30 000 tonnes a year of the material is extracted for this product.
   a) How long will the world stocks now last?
   b) When will the stocks now run out?

18 Imagine a recycling programme has been set up in which 200 000 tonnes of the material in question 16 could be recycled each year.
   a) How long would the stocks now last using:
      i) 250 000 tonnes a year,
      ii) 280 000 tonnes a year?
   b) What effect does the recycling programme have on the reserves of the material?

19 If 1000 million tonnes of bauxite is mined every year and it is estimated that stocks will last until about 2240, how much bauxite is on the Earth?

20 What are the benefits of recycling?

**Figure 12.15**  Recycling centre.

## Materials and energy

The processing of all materials needs energy and this is provided mainly by the fossil fuels – coal, oil and natural gas. These are non-renewable raw materials and while stocks of coal may only last until the year 2300, stocks of oil and natural gas are predicted to be used up in your lifetime, if used at the present rate. When materials are recycled there is a reduction in the amount of energy used to make the new products. Although some energy is used in the recycling process, it is usually less than the energy used in extraction.

## Using materials in the future

Increasing amounts of many materials are being recycled and new ways are being found to save energy in chemical processing to meet the demands of the human population, today and in the future. New materials are made every year through investigations into the way different chemicals react together. From these discoveries, materials are selected which can perform a task more efficiently than an existing material and require smaller amounts of raw materials and energy. In the long term, there are plans to set up mines on the Moon to extract minerals and to process them, to make materials in space for use on Earth and in further space exploration.

21  When oil and natural gas supplies are used up, do you think the stocks of coal will still be expected to last until 2300? Explain your answer.

22  How does the recycling of materials affect the stocks of fossil fuels? Explain your answer.

**Figure 12.16**  Impression of a NASA lunar base showing mining operations.

# ◆ SUMMARY ◆

◆ From the earliest civilisations human activity has caused some pollution but the problem greatly increased with the Industrial Revolution *(see page 151)*.

◆ Air is polluted by solid particles and by chemicals *(see page 153)*.

◆ There are a number of ways in which air quality can be improved *(see page 157)*.

◆ Fresh water may be polluted with dangerous heavy metals *(see page 159)*.

◆ Sea water may be polluted with oil *(see page 160)*.

◆ Some pesticides, rubbish and the extraction of raw materials damage the land environment *(see page 161)*.

◆ Some materials are renewable while others are non-renewable *(see page 163)*.

◆ Recycling conserves stocks of raw materials, including fuels *(see page 164)*.

## *End of chapter question*

1  Using the information in this chapter, what policies would you suggest to the governments of all countries to improve the quality of the world environment and ensure that future generations have the resources they need to meet their needs?

# 13 | *The periodic table*

In Chapter 4 it was shown that the substances from which things are made can be broken down into elements. Each element has a chemical symbol and is made of atoms. Inside an atom is a nucleus containing protons and neutrons, surrounded by electrons.

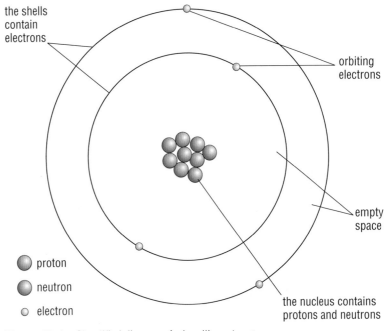

**Figure 13.1** Simplified diagram of a beryllium atom.

## Sorting out the elements

John Dalton (1766–1844) was an English chemist who tried to sort the elements into an order. He decided to compare their weights. He measured the weights of the elements he collected when he broke up compounds. He used the weight of hydrogen to compare with the weight of the other elements. For example, when he separated hydrogen and oxygen from the compound water he found that the weight of oxygen was seven times greater than the weight of hydrogen. As he believed that one atom of hydrogen combined with one atom of oxygen to make a molecule of water he thought that the atomic weight of hydrogen was one and the atomic weight of oxygen was seven. He used this idea to measure the atomic weights of the elements and set them out in a table.

**Figure A** The symbols for atoms used by Dalton.

*(continued)*

Unfortunately Dalton was not a very accurate experimenter and other scientists found that the weight of oxygen produced when water is split up is eight times greater than the weight of hydrogen, so they thought that its atomic weight should be eight. However, Dalton had also made a mistake in thinking that all atoms combine in the ratio of 1 to 1.

It was later discovered that a molecule of water contains two atoms of hydrogen combined with one atom of oxygen. This means that the weight of an oxygen atom is eight times the weight of two hydrogen atoms, or 16 times the weight of one atom – making its atomic weight 16, not 8. There were many revisions of the idea of atomic weights (today we use the term relative atomic mass or RAM) but atomic weights helped scientists to sort out the elements into an order which could be studied further.

John Newlands (1838–1898) set out the elements in order of atomic weight, starting with the lowest. When he looked at some of the elements that were eight spaces apart he discovered that they had similar properties. Moving down the list in this way he found that some of the properties re-appeared periodically.

Dmitri Mendeleev (1834–1907) also noticed how the properties of the elements varied periodically and rearranged the elements into a table known as the periodic table (see below). He found that elements in the columns had similar properties and he called these columns of elements groups. Mendeleev assumed that there were still elements to be discovered and so left gaps in the table where he thought they would eventually be placed. He could predict the properties of the missing elements from the arrangement of the elements in the table. Eventually the missing elements were discovered and were found to have the properties that Mendeleev predicted. Over the years the periodic table has been revised. Today the elements are arranged in order of atomic number (see opposite). Elements in different areas of the periodic table have specific properties.

1 Dalton made mistakes, but in what way was his work useful in sorting out the elements?
2 What did Newlands and Mendeleev see in the table of atomic weights?
3 How did the discoveries of elements made after Mendeleev had produced his table show him to be right?

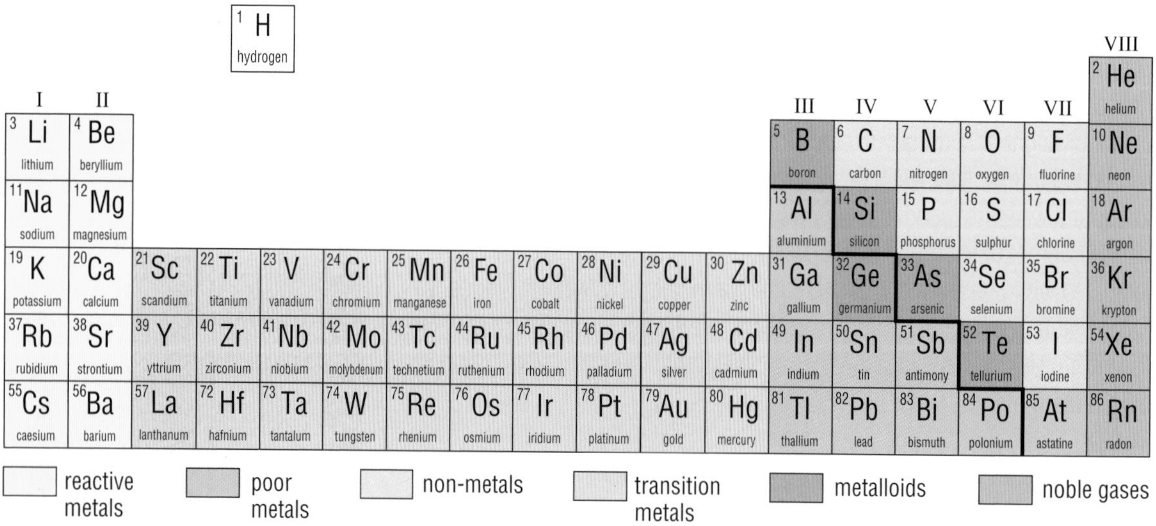

**Figure 13.2**  Part of the modern periodic table.

# Atomic number

In the nucleus of each atom of each element there is a certain number of protons. This number is different from the number of protons in the nuclei of any other element's atoms. The number of protons in an atom is called the atomic number. Elements are arranged in order of their atomic number in the periodic table.

# Groups of the periodic table

Many of the columns of elements in the periodic table are called groups. The elements in a group share similar properties. A trend can be seen in the properties as you go down the group.

## Group I, the alkali metals

The metals in this group are not alkalis, but the oxides and hydroxides that they form are. It is this property of these compounds that gives the metals in this group their name.

Table 13.1 shows some of the physical properties of the alkali metals.

**Table 13.1**   Physical properties of the alkali metals.

| Element | Density g/cm$^3$ | Melting point °C | Boiling point °C |
|---------|------------------|------------------|------------------|
| Lithium | 0.53 | 180.6 | 1344 |
| Sodium | 0.97 | 97.9 | 884 |
| Potassium | 0.86 | 63.5 | 760 |
| Rubidium | 1.53 | 39.3 | 688 |
| Caesium | 1.90 | 28.5 | 671 |

## *A closer look at the alkali metals*

### Lithium

Lithium's name is derived from lithis, the Greek word for stone, because it is found in many kinds of igneous rock. It is used in batteries and in compounds used as medicines to treat mental disorders.

### Sodium

Metallic sodium is used in certain kinds of street lamp that give an orange glow. It is alloyed with potassium to make a material for transferring heat in a nuclear reactor. Sodium compounds such as sodium hydroxide have a wide range of uses (see Chapter 11 page 142). In the body sodium is needed by nerve cells. They use it in the transfer of electrical signals called nerve impulses.

### Potassium

Potassium is used to make the fertiliser potassium nitrate. In the body it is used for the control of the water content of the blood and is used with sodium in sending electrical signals by nerve cells.

1 Which of these statements about the trends in Table 13.1 are true?

  **a)** The density of the metals generally **i)** increases, **ii)** decreases down the group.

  **b)** The melting point of the metals generally **i)** increases, **ii)** decreases down the group.

  **c)** The boiling point of the metals generally **i)** increases, **ii)** decreases down the group.

2 Which element does not follow a trend? Describe how it differs from the trend.

3 Sodium is a softer metal than lithium. Describe how you think the softness of potassium and rubidium compare with that of sodium.

4 Which metal has the smallest temperature range for its liquid form?

5 Look at the information about sodium and potassium in the reactivity series (Table 9.2 page 111) and predict a position for **a)** lithium and **b)** rubidium in the series.

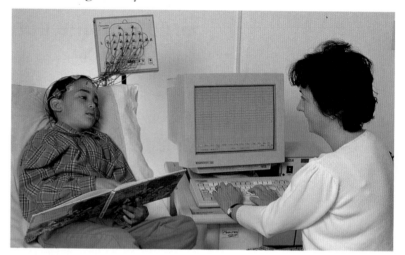

**Figure 13.2** Measuring brain waves – nerve impulses are due to the movement of sodium and potassium ions in brain cells.

### Rubidium

Rubidium gets its name from the Latin word ruber, which means red. This describes the lines produced by rubidium when it is examined with a device called a spectroscope. Rubidium is used in the filaments of photo-electric cells which convert light energy into electrical energy.

### Caesium

Caesium's name comes from the Latin word caesius, which means bluish-grey. This describes the colour of the lines the metal produces when examined with a spectroscope. Caesium is used in photo-electric cells and as a time keeper in atomic clocks. The vibration of the atoms is used to measure time very accurately. Each atom vibrates over nine thousand million times a second.

## Group II, the alkaline earth metals

These metals are not alkalis but their oxides and hydroxides dissolve slightly in water to make alkaline solutions. Table 13.2 shows some of the physical properties of these metals.

**6** Which of these statements about the trends in Table 13.2 are true?

**a)** The density of the metals generally **i)** increases, **ii)** decreases down the group.

**b)** The melting point of the metals generally **i)** increases, **ii)** decreases down the group.

**c)** The boiling point of the metals generally **i)** increases, **ii)** decreases down the group.

*For discussion*

How do the trends shown in Table 13.2 compare with those shown in Table 13.1?

**Table 13.2** Properties of the alkaline earth metals.

| Element | Density g/cm³ | Melting point °C | Boiling point °C |
|---------|---------------|------------------|------------------|
| Beryllium | 1.85 | 1289 | 2476 |
| Magnesium | 1.74 | 649 | 1097 |
| Calcium | 1.53 | 840 | 1493 |
| Strontium | 2.58 | 768 | 1387 |
| Barium | 3.60 | 729 | 1880 |

## A closer look at the alkaline earth metals

### Beryllium

Beryllium combines with aluminium, silicon and oxygen to make a mineral called beryl. Emerald and aquamarine are two varieties of beryl which are used as gemstones in jewellery.

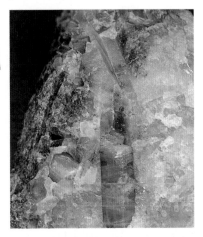 

**Figure 13.3** Emerald (left) and aquamarine (right).

Beryllium is mixed with other metals to make alloys that are strong, yet light in weight. It is also used in a mechanism that controls the speed of neutron particles in a nuclear reactor.

### Magnesium

Magnesium is used in fireworks to make a brilliant white light. Another important use is to mix it with other metals to make strong, lightweight alloys such as those used to make bicycle frames.

Green plants need magnesium in order to make the chlorophyll that traps the energy from sunlight in photosynthesis. Magnesium is needed in the body for the formation of healthy bones and teeth.

### Calcium

Calcium's name is derived from the word calx, which is the Latin name for the substance lime. Lime is actually calcium oxide. Calcium forms many compounds with a wide range of uses, from baking powders and bleaching powders to medicines and plastics. In the human body calcium is required for the formation of healthy teeth and bones and for the contraction of muscles.

### Strontium

Strontium forms salts which make a red flame when they burn. They are used in flares for signalling the position of survivors of shipwrecks and to make the red colour in fireworks. Strontium has radioactive isotopes which are produced in nuclear reactions.

**Figure 13.4** A flare set off on a training exercise.

### Barium

Barium has a wide range of uses, from safety matches and providing the green colour in fireworks to mixing with other metals to make alloys. It is best known in a form called a barium meal. This substance is barium sulphate and it forms a suspension that stops X-rays passing through it.

A barium meal is used in medicine to examine the alimentary canal of a patient. The patient eats the barium meal and as it passes along the alimentary canal, the patient's body is X-rayed. The outline of the alimentary canal and the position of the barium meal can be seen in the X-ray photographs. The pictures help the doctors to diagnose the patient's condition.

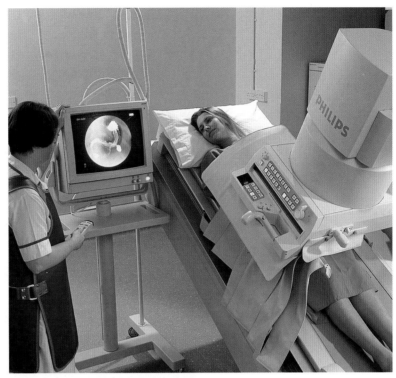

**Figure 13.5** Examining an X-ray of a patient's abdomen using a barium meal.

# Group VII, the halogens

The word halogen is a Greek word for salt former and all the elements in this group form salts readily. Table 13.3 shows some of the properties of these elements.

7 What trends can you see in the melting points and the boiling points of the halogens?

8 Using the information in the table deduce which halogens are **a)** solids, **b)** liquids and **c)** gases at room temperature. Explain your answers.

9 Fluorine is more reactive than chlorine, chlorine is more reactive than bromine and bromine is more reactive than iodine. Is this trend shared by the alkali metals and alkaline earth metals? Explain your answer. (Look at the reactivity series, Table 9.2 on page 111, to help you answer.)

**Table 13.3**

| Element | Melting point °C | Boiling point °C |
|---------|------------------|------------------|
| Fluorine | −219.7 | −188.2 |
| Chlorine | −100.9 | −34.0 |
| Bromine | −7.3 | 59.1 |
| Iodine | 113.6 | 185.3 |
| Astatine | 302 | 377 |

## *A closer look at the halogens*

### Fluorine

Fluorine is a pale yellow–green poisonous gas. It is found in combination with calcium in the mineral fluorite. This mineral glows weakly when ultraviolet light is shone on it. This property is called fluorescence. One variety of fluorite called Blue John has coloured bands and is carved into ornaments.

Fluorine is combined with hydrogen to make hydrogen fluoride which dissolves glass and is used in etching glass surfaces. Sodium fluoride prevents tooth decay and is added to some drinking water supplies. Fluorine is one of the elements in CFCs.

**Figure 13.6** Fluorite glowing.

## Chlorine

Chlorine is a yellow–green poisonous gas. It is found in combination with sodium as rock salt. Chlorine is used to kill bacteria in water supply systems and is also used in the manufacture of bleach. It forms hydrochloric acid which has many uses in industry.

## Bromine

Bromine is a red–brown liquid which produces a brown vapour at room temperature that has a strong smell and is poisonous. Bromine is extracted from bromide salts in sea water and is used, with silver, in photography. Silver bromide is light sensitive and is used in photographic film to record the amount of light in different parts of the image focused by the camera lens.

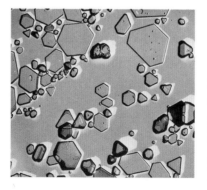 

**Figure 13.7** Magnified images showing silver bromide crystals on a piece of photographic film (left) and silver deposits on a developed film (right).

### Iodine

Iodine is a grey–black solid. It is extracted from iodine salts in sea water and is used as an antiseptic and also in photography. Potassium iodide solution is used to detect starch in food tests. It is needed by the body for the production of a hormone which acts as a catalyst in oxidation reactions in the cells.

### Astatine

This element is radioactive. It has many isotopes but they are all unstable and eventually break down into other elements.

## ◆ SUMMARY ◆

- The elements are arranged in order of their atomic number in the periodic table *(see page 168)*.
- The atomic number of an element is the number of protons in the nucleus of its atoms *(see page 169)*.
- Group I of the periodic table contains the alkali metals *(see page 169)*.
- Group II of the periodic table contains the alkaline earth metals *(see page 170)*.
- Group VII of the periodic table contains the halogens *(see page 173)*.

## *End of chapter question*

**1** Elements in the alkali metals, alkaline earth metals and halogens are important in our lives. How accurate is this statement? Explain your answer.

# 14 Using formulae

The origins of the symbols used in formulae are described on page 54. The symbols of most of the elements are shown in the periodic table on page 168.

The symbols are used to write formulae for elements or the compounds that the elements form. Often a number is featured in the formula. It is below the line of the letters. This number indicates the number of atoms of the element which is immediately to the left of it. For example, oxygen exists as oxygen molecules. Each one is formed from two oxygen atoms. The formula for the oxygen molecule is $O_2$. Other examples of molecules made from two atoms of one element are chlorine, $Cl_2$, and hydrogen, $H_2$.

A molecule of carbon dioxide has one atom of carbon and two atoms of oxygen. Its formula is $CO_2$.

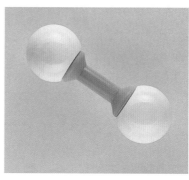
Hydrogen

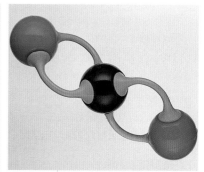
Carbon dioxide

**Figure 14.1** Plastic spheres can be connected together to make models of molecules.

1 Write the formula for:
   a) sodium hydroxide (it has one atom each of sodium, oxygen and hydrogen),
   b) sodium nitrate (it has one atom of sodium and nitrogen and three atoms of oxygen),
   c) sodium sulphate (it has two atoms of sodium, one atom of sulphur and four atoms of oxygen).
2 Sometimes the name of a compound gives a clue to its formula. What do you think is the formula of
   a) sulphur dioxide,
   b) carbon monoxide?
3 What does the formula equation tell you that the word equation does not?

Some molecules have three or more elements in them and there may be a different number of atoms of each element. For example, in a molecule of sulphuric acid there are two atoms of hydrogen, one atom of sulphur and four atoms of oxygen. The formula for sulphuric acid is $H_2SO_4$.

Calcium hydroxide is unusual in that an atom of calcium is combined with two hydroxide ions and each ion is made from an oxygen and a hydrogen atom. In this case brackets are used around the hydroxide ion and the figure 2 is put beside them to show that two hydroxide ions are present. The formula for calcium hydroxide is $Ca(OH)_2$.

The word equation used to describe a chemical reaction can be replaced by an equation using the formulae of the compounds involved. This equation allows you to write down information about the reaction more quickly. It also allows more information to be given about how the atoms of the elements combine. For example, the reaction between calcium and chlorine can be written as:

calcium + chlorine → calcium chloride

$$Ca + Cl_2 → CaCl_2$$

Care must be taken when substituting formulae for words as the number of atoms of each element on one side of the equation must be the same as the number on the other side. To make the numbers balance, other numbers may have to be added in front of one or more of the formulae for the reactants and products. For example:

calcium + oxygen → calcium oxide

$$Ca + O_2 → CaO$$

In this form there are two atoms of oxygen on the left and only one on the right. The equation is balanced by adding a 2 in front of the CaO to balance the oxygen atoms and by adding a 2 in front of the Ca to balance the calcium atoms. The balanced equation is:

$$2Ca + O_2 → 2CaO$$

When balancing equations, the formulae of the reactants and products must not be altered. For example:

sodium + chlorine → sodium chloride

$$Na + Cl_2 → NaCl$$

The equation is not balanced and although it could be balanced by making $NaCl_2$, this compound is not formed and the equation would be incorrect.

The equation can only be balanced by making it:

$$2Na + Cl_2 → 2NaCl$$

**4** Check these equations and balance them if necessary:
 **a)** $H_2 + I_2 → HI$,
 **b)** $2C + O_2 → 2CO$,
 **c)** $K + H_2O → KOH + H_2$,
 **d)** $Mg + O_2 → 2MgO$,
 **e)** $KI → 2K + I_2$,
 **f)** $CuO + H_2SO_4$
   $→ CuSO_4 + H_2O$,
 **g)** $H_2O_2 → H_2O + O_2$.

**Figure 14.2** By studying reactions carefully, the structure of large molecules can be discovered.

5  When solid zinc oxide is placed in an aqueous solution of hydrochloric acid, zinc chloride is produced which dissolves in the water. Water is also produced.
   **a)** Write the word equation for this reaction.
   **b)** Write the formula equation for this reaction using the formulae in this list – HCl, $ZnCl_2$, $H_2O$, ZnO.
   **c)** Balance the equation.
   **d)** Write in the state symbols.

# State symbols

The chemicals taking part in the reaction and the products that they form may be in different states of matter. These states can be represented by symbols in the equation. In addition to (s) for solid, (l) for liquid and (g) for gas there is a fourth symbol. It is (aq) and shows that the chemical is in an aqueous solution, which means that it is dissolved in water. The symbols are added after the formula for each chemical. For example:

$$\text{calcium carbonate} + \text{hydrochloric acid} \rightarrow \text{calcium chloride} + \text{water} + \text{carbon dioxide}$$

$$CaCO_3(s) + 2HCl(aq) \rightarrow CaCl_2(aq) + H_2O(l) + CO_2(g)$$

## ◆ SUMMARY ◆

◆ Word equations can be replaced by formula equations *(see page 176)*.
◆ Formula equations must be balanced *(see page 177)*.
◆ State symbols are added to formula equations to provide information about the states of the reactants and products *(see page 178)*.

### *End of chapter question*

1  Use the information in this chapter and the data in appropriate tables to construct balanced equations for other reactions in this book.

# Glossary

## A

**acid**   A substance with a pH less than 7.0 that reacts with metals to produce hydrogen.

**acid rain**   Rain produced by the reaction of sulphur dioxide and oxides of nitrogen with water in clouds. It has a pH of less than 5.

**alchemy**   The ancient study of chemical reactions to produce gold from less expensive metals, or to produce a chemical that would extend life.

**alkali**   A base that is soluble in water and makes an alkaline solution.

**alkaline**   A condition of a liquid in which the pH is greater than 7.

**allotrope**   One of two or more forms in which an element can exist. For example, carbon can exist as diamond, graphite or buckminster-fullerene.

**alloy**   A mixture of two or more metals, or of a metal such as iron with a non-metal such as carbon.

**atom**   A particle of an element that can take part in a chemical reaction. It contains a central nucleus which is surrounded by electrons.

## B

**base**   A substance that can take part in a chemical reaction with an acid, forming a salt and water.

**boiling**   A process in which a liquid turns to a vapour at the liquid's boiling point.

**boiling point**   The highest temperature to which a liquid can be heated before the liquid turns into a gas.

## C

**cell**   A device which contains chemicals that react and produce a current of electricity in a closed circuit.

**centrifuge**   A machine that separates substances of different densities in a mixture by spinning them in test-tubes.

**chromatography**   A process in which substances dissolved in a liquid are separated from each other by allowing the liquid to flow through porous paper.

**combustion**   A chemical reaction in which a substance combines with oxygen quickly and heat is given out in the process. If a flame is produced, burning is said to take place.

**compound**   A substance made from the atoms of two or more elements that have joined together by taking part in a chemical reaction.

**condensation**   A process in which a gas cools and changes into a liquid.

**cracking**   A process in which hydrocarbons with large molecules are broken down into smaller hydrocarbon molecules.

**crystal**   A substance made from an orderly arrangement of atoms or molecules that produces flat surfaces, arranged at certain angles to each other.

**crystallisation**   A process in which crystals are formed from a liquid or a gas.

## D

**decant**   A process of separating a liquid from its sediment by pouring the liquid away from the sediment.

**decomposition**   A chemical reaction breaking down a substance into simpler substances.

**density**   The mass of a substance that is found in a certain volume.

**diffusion**   A process in which the particles in two gases or two liquids, or the particles of a solute in a solvent, mix on their own without being stirred.

**displacement**   A reaction in which a metal in a salt is replaced by another metal.

**distillate**   A liquid produced by distillation.

**distillation**   A process of separating a solute from a solvent by heating the solution they make, until the solvent turns into a gas and is condensed and collected separately without the solute.

## E

**electrolysis**   The process in which a chemical decomposition occurs due to the passage of electricity through an electrolyte.

**electrolyte**   A solution or molten solid through which a current of electricity can pass.

**electron**   A tiny particle in an atom which moves round the nucleus. It has a negative electric charge.

**element**   A substance made of one type of atom. It cannot be split up by chemical reactions into simpler substances.

**evaporation**   A process in which a liquid turns into a gas without boiling.

## F

**fermentation**   The process in which sugar is broken down by yeast to produce alcohol and carbon dioxide.

**filtration**   A process of separation of solid particles from a liquid by passing the liquid through paper with small holes in it.

**fractional distillation**   The separation of liquids with different boiling points in a mixture by distillation.

## G

**gas**   A substance with a volume that changes to fill any container into which it is poured.

## H

**hydrocarbon**   A compound made from hydrogen and carbon only.

## I

**igneous rock**   Rock formed by the cooling of magma inside the Earth's crust or lava on the surface of the crust.

**immiscible**   A property of a liquid that does not allow it to mix with another liquid.

**incandescence**   The glowing of a substance, due to the amount of heat that it has received.

## L

**liquid**   A substance with a definite volume that flows and takes up the shape of any container into which it is poured.

## M

**magma**   Hot liquid rock in the mantle and in some parts of the crust of the Earth.

**mantle**   A hot layer of rock beneath the Earth's crust.

**mass**   The amount of matter in a substance. It is measured in units such as grams and kilograms.

**metal**   A member of a group of elements which are shiny, good conductors of heat and electricity and displace hydrogen from dilute acids.

**metamorphic rock**   Rock formed by the effect of heat and pressure on igneous or sedimentary rock.

**mineral**   A substance that has formed from an element or compound in the Earth and exists separately, or with other minerals to form rocks.

**miscible**   A property of a liquid that allows it to mix freely with another liquid.

**molecule**   A group of atoms joined together that may be identical, in the molecules of an element, or different, in the molecules of a compound.

## N

**neutralisation**   A reaction between an acid and a base in which the products (salt and water) do not have the properties of the reactants.

**neutron**   A particle in the nucleus of an atom that has no electrical charge.

**non-metal**   A member of a group of elements that are not shiny and do not conduct heat or electricity, or displace hydrogen from dilute acids.

**nucleus**   The central part of an atom, which contains particles called protons and neutrons.

## O

**ore**   A rocky material that is rich in a mineral from which a metal can be extracted.

**oxidation**   A reaction in which oxygen is added to a substance, or hydrogen is removed from it.

## P

**periodic table**   The arrangement of the elements in order of their atomic number that allows elements with similar properties to be grouped together.

**precipitate**   Particles of a solid that form in a liquid or a gas as a result of a chemical reaction.

**precipitation**   The process of forming a precipitate in a liquid or a gas.

**pressure**   A measurement of a force that is acting over a certain area.

**products**   The substances that are produced when a chemical reaction takes place.

**proton**   A particle in the nucleus of an atom that has a positive electrical charge.

## R

**reactants**   The substances that take part in a chemical reaction.

**reactivity series**   The arrangement of metals in order of their reactivity with oxygen, water and acids, starting with the most reactive metal.

**reduction**   A chemical reaction in which oxygen is taken from a substance, or hydrogen is added to it.

**reversible reaction**   A chemical reaction which can be reversed. The products of the reaction become the reactants of the reverse reaction.

### S

**salt**   A compound that is formed when an acid reacts with a substance such as a metal, or when an acid reacts with a base.

**sediment**   A collection of solid particles that settle out from a mixture of a solid and a liquid.

**sedimentary rock**   Rock formed by particles settling out of suspensions in lakes and seas.

**solid**   A substance that has a definite shape and volume.

**soluble**   A property of a substance that allows it to dissolve in a solvent.

**solute**   A substance that can dissolve in a solvent.

**solution**   A liquid that is made from a solute and a solvent.

**solvent**   A liquid in which a solute can dissolve.

**spectroscope**   An instrument for examining the light produced by an element when it is strongly heated.

**sublimation**   A process in which a solid turns into a gas, or a gas turns into a solid. There is no liquid stage in this process.

**suspension**   A collection of tiny, solid particles that are spread out through a liquid or a gas.

**synthesis**   A chemical reaction in which a substance is made from other substances.

### T

**temperature**   A measure of the hotness or coldness of a substance.

# *Index*

acid rain 101, 155
acids 65, 69–71, 109
   detecting 72–3
   strong and weak 73
acrylic plastics 133
aerosols 18, 35, 159
air 15, 19, 20, 77–90
   composition 18
   improving quality of 157–9
   liquid 78–9
   pollution 101, 153-9
   uses of gases 79–82
alchemist's symbols 54–5
alchemy 1, 48
alcoholic drinks 66
alkali metals (Group I) 169–70
alkaline earth metals (Group II) 170–3
alkalis 71–3, 105
allotropes 104, 133
alloys 121
aluminium 89, 120, 131–2, 162
   electrolysis of 118, 131–2
   extraction 164
   properties and uses 132
aluminium bronze 132
aluminium cell 131–2
aluminium hydroxide 131
aluminium oxide 131
aluminium silicate 131
ammonia 28, 80, 87, 144–5, 158
ammonia plant 144
ammonium sulphate 142, 158
andesitic volcano 93, 103
anode 115, 123
antioxidants 67, 90
apparatus 6–9, 12–14
aquamarine 171
Archeson process 133
argentum 56
argon 78, 80–1
astatine 175
atmosphere 77, 152–3
atomic number 169
atomic theory 51–2
atomic weight 167–8
atoms, basic structure 52–4, 167

bacteria, use of nitrates by 153
barium 172
barium meal 172–3
barium sulphate 172
basalt 93, 94, 95
basaltic volcano 93, 94, 103
bases 65, 71–2, 105
batch process 140

battery 113
bauxite 131
beryl 96, 171
beryllium 171
Berzelius, Jöns Jakob 55
Black, Joseph 87
blast furnace 126–7
Blue John 173
boiling 20–1, 25
boiling point 21, 29, 31, 43
Boltzmann, Ludwig 30
borosilicate glass 6
Bosch, Karl 144
Boyle, Robert 30, 47, 55
brake fluid 17
brass 125
brine 142
bromine 51, 56, 116, 143, 174–5
bronze 124, 127
Bronze Age 124, 150
Buchner funnel 40
buckminsterfullerene 133, 135
bucky ball 135
bulb, thermometer 4, 5
Bunsen, Robert 7
Bunsen burner 7–8, 84–5
burette 2, 3
burning 80, 82–4
burning glass 87

cadmium 159
caesium 170
calcium 108, 172
calcium carbonate 59, 60, 100, 127
calcium chloride 118, 177
calcium hydroxide 60, 108, 176
calcium oxide 59, 60, 105, 127, 177
calcium silicate 127
calcium sulphate 101, 142
calx 88, 172
carbon 54, 104, 115, 133–5
carbon dioxide 66, 100
   as air pollution 153, 154
   formation 106, 127
   solid 21, 26
   test for 60
carbon monoxide 84, 127
   as air pollution 153, 154
carbonates 133
Carlisle, Anthony 113
cast iron 128, 132
catalyst 67
catalytic converters 159
cathode 115, 123
Celsius scale 5

centrifuge 40
CFCs (chlorofluorocarbons) 153, 154, 174
chalcopyrite 123
chalk 97
charcoal 133, 135
chemical engineers 140
chemical equations 57, 176–8
chemical industry 139–49
chemical plant 14, 139, 140,.148
chemical reactions 57–67
   energy and 57–8
   speed of 67
   types 58–66
chemical symbols 54–6
chemical weathering 99, 100–1
chlorine 51, 56, 143, 174
chromatogram 42
chromatography 42
chromatography tank 42
chromium 89, 159
chromium plating 90
clay 34
clouds 22
coal 162
cobalt chloride 62
coke 135, 159
combustion 82–8
compounds 33–5, 47–52, 96
concentration and reaction speed 67
condensation 21, 26, 43
conductor of heat 104
Contact process 141
continental crust 93
copper 96, 123–5, 162
   extraction 123–4
   plating copper on 118–19
   properties 107, 108, 109, 124
   pure 124
   purification 164
   reaction with oxygen 107
   uses 124
   world stocks 163
copper carbonate, decomposition of 61
copper oxide 62, 65
copper pyrites 123
copper sulphate 110
   anhydrous 61, 62
   decomposition of crystals 61
   electrolysis of 116
   hydrated 61, 62
   solution 115
copper sulphide 105
cracking 147
creosote 141
cryolite 131

crystal 41, 92, 95, 96, 98, 101
crystallisation 41
cubic centimetres 2, 3
cyclohexane 36

Dalton, John 51, 52, 167–8
Davy, Humphry 113
DDT 161
decanting 39
decomposition 58–63
    by electricity 63
    by light 62–3
    thermal 58–62
Democritus 30, 51
dephlogisticated air 88
detergents 142
diamond 96, 105, 133, 134–5
diffusion 31
displacement reactions 65–6, 109–10
dissolving 35
distillation 8, 9, 43, 44–5, 145–7
distillation tower 145
Down's cell 118
dry cell 112, 144
dry ice 21

Earth (planet) 28, 91–103
    changing atmosphere 152–3
    crust 92–3
    plates in mantle 102–3
    structure 91–4
earth 20
earthquakes 91
einsteinium 56
electrical conduction 104
electricity 131, 153
    decomposition and 63
    generating with metals 111–14
    passage through different substances
        114–15
    use in chemistry 112–13
electrodes 115
electrolysis 113, 115–19
    extraction of metals by 117–18
    of non-metals 118
    of solutions 116–17
electrolyte, pure molten 116
electrons 52–3
electroplated nickel silver (EPNS) 119, 123
electroplating 118–19
electrostatic precipitator 158
elements 47–52
    discovery of 48–50
    Greek 19–20
    properties 50–1
emeralds 96, 171
emulsion 34

energy 165
    chemical reactions and 57–8
    heat 24, 33, 164
environment, chemicals and 150–66
enzymes 67
ethanoic acid 70
ethanol 36, 37, 66, 70, 115
    distillation of 44–5
evaporation 20–1, 22, 25, 41
expanding 24
extrusive igneous rock 95

Faraday, Michael 113
fermentation 66, 70
ferrum 56
fertilisers 160
filtrate 40
filtration 39–40
fire 19, 20
    triangle of 85–6
fire blanket 86
fire extinguisher 75, 76
fire fighters 85–6
fire rocks 95
fireworks 64, 171
flotation cell 38, 123, 125
fluorescence 173
fluorine 173–4
foam 35, 86
fog 35
food spoilage, controlling 90
formula equations 57
formulae 176–8
fractional distillation 43, 145–7
fractionating column 78
Frasch, Herman 136
freezing 20, 25
freezing point 20
Fuller, Buckminster 135

galena 125
Galvani, Luigi 112
galvanising 90
gas 15, 86
    collecting over water 87
    compressed 18
    forces of attraction in 24
    natural 83, 84, 145
    pressure in 27
    properties 16
gas/liquid mixtures 35
gas sylvestre 86
gemstones 96, 171
germanium crystals 81
glass 164
gloss paint 37
gold 54, 96, 121–2
    changing lead into 1
    extraction 121

    precipitation of 121
    properties and uses 122
    reaction with oxygen 107
granite 93, 95
graphite 104, 105, 133–4
greenhouse effect 154
greenhouse gases 154
ground-glass joints 12, 13
gypsum 98

Haber, Fritz 144
Haber process 144
habitat destruction 162, 163
haematite 126
Hales, Stephen 87
halogens (Group VII) 173–5
hazard symbols 69, 71
heat energy 24, 33, 164
helium 81
Helmont, Joannes Baptista van 86
Hero 30
hot spots 94
hydrocarbons 145
hydrochloric acid 65, 70, 109, 174
hydrogen 52
    apparatus for collection of 71
    in atmosphere 77
    ions 73
    reactivity of 117
    solid 28
    test for 108
hydrogen fluoride 174
hydroxide ions 73

ice 25, 27
igneous rock 95–7, 98
immiscible liquid 36
    separating 45–6
Industrial Revolution 151
insoluble solid/gas 36
insoluble solid/liquid mixture, separating
    399–40
insulator 104
intrusive igneous rock 95
iodine 26, 175, 104
ions 54, 73
iron 56, 92, 126–30
    cast 128, 132
    early workers in 127–8
    extraction 59, 120, 126–7, 164
    pig 127
    reaction with acid 109
    reaction with oxygen 107
    reaction with water 89, 108
    uses 133
    world stocks 163
    wrought 128
iron oxide 88, 126

iron sulphate 110
iron sulphide 64
isotopes 54

Jupiter 28

kalium 56
kimberlite 134
krypton 78, 82

laboratory rules 9–12
land, pollution on 161–2
lattice 23
lava 93
Lavoisier, Antoine 47, 51, 52, 55, 88
law of conservation of mass 51
law of definite proportions 52
leaching 155
lead 109, 125–6, 159
    changing into gold 1
    extraction 125
    as pollutant 156–7
    properties and uses 125–6
lead bromide 116
lead sulphide 125
lichens 72
Liebig, Justus von 8, 9
Liebig condenser 8, 44
light emitting diode (LED) 111
lime 60, 75, 172
limelight 59
limestone 100, 125
    decomposition of 58, 59, 98
    formation 97
    uses 59–60
Linde, Karl von 78
liquid 15
    forces of attraction in 24
    pressure in 26
    properties 16
    pure 115
liquid/gas mixtures 35
liquid/liquid mixtures 34
lithium 169
litmus 65, 72
luminous flame 85

magma 92, 101
magnesium 92, 106, 108, 109, 171
magnesium carbonate 100
magnesium hydroxide 108
magnesium oxide 62, 64, 106
magnesium sulphate 101, 117
magnetic field 92
magnetic separator 37–8, 164
magnets 130
marble 98, 99
Mars 91

mass 15, 16, 22
matter
    changing states 20–2, 24–6
    first ideas about 19–20
    fourth state of 54
    interaction of states of 23
    particles of 23–4
    properties 15–20
    structure of 30
    using properties of 16–18
Maxwell, James Clerk 30
measuring
    mass of a solid or liquid 3–4
    temperature 4–5
    volume of a gas 3
    volumes of liquids 2
measuring cylinder 2–3
melting 20, 24
melting point 20, 31
Mendeleev, Dmitri 168
meniscus 2–3
mercury 115
    meniscus of 3
    properties 51, 104
    in thermometer 3, 4
metal oxides 62,105
metals 70, 107–14, 120–33
    chemical properties 105–6
    extraction of 117–18
    physical properties 104–5
    plating one with another 118–19
metamorphic rock 98–9
meteorological balloons 81
methane 28, 65, 84, 161–2
methanoic acid 74
milk 34
millilitres 2, 3
mineral acids 70
minerals 96–7
mining 162, 165, 166
miscibility 36
miscible liquids 36
    separating 44–5
mist 35
mixtures 33–5
    separating 37–46

nanotechnology 16
native elements 96, 120
natrium 56
natural gas 83, 84, 145
neon 78, 81
neutralisation 65, 74–6
neutrons 52, 54
Newlands, John 168
Nicholson, William 113
nickel 92, 159
nitrates 79, 153

nitric acid 70, 80, 144, 145
nitrogen 51, 88
    in food spoilage control 90
    liquid 79
    production by bacteria 153
    uses of 79–80
nitrogen dioxide 79
nitrogen oxides as air pollution 153, 155
noble gases 78, 80–2
non-luminous flame 85
non-metals 133–7
    chemical properties 105–6
    electrolysis of 118
    physical properties 104–5
non-renewable materials 163–5
nuclear power stations 95
nucleus 52

oceanic crust 93
oil
    in engines 17
    pollution 160–1
    in rust prevention 90
oleum 141
opal 96
open cast mining 162
ore 38, 120
organic acids 70
out-gassing 77
oxidation 64–5, 70, 82
oxides 106
oxygen 51, 88, 92
    action on metal surfaces 89
    atomic weight 167–8
    production by plants 152
    reactions of metals with 107
    reactions with 105–6
    test for 83
    uses of 80
    in water 37
oxygen furnace 129–30
ozone 153, 156
ozone layer 153

paint 34
paint remover 36
paper 164
particle theory of matter 23
pelican 47
periodic table 106, 167–75
    groups of 169–75
    origins of 168
peroxyacetyl nitrate (PAN) 156
petrochemical industry 145–7
petrol, unleaded 159
petroleum 145
pewter 126
pH meter 73

pH scale 73, 74
philosopher's stone 1
phlogiston theory 86–8
phosphates 160
photography 62, 174–5
photosynthesis 58
physical weathering 99–100
pig iron 127
plasma 54
plastics 132–3
platinum 115, 159
pollution 151–2
    air 101, 153–9
    land 161–2
    water 159–61
polychlorinated biphenyls (PCBs) 159
polypropylene plastics 133
polythene 133
pot holes 100
potassium 56, 109, 113, 170
potassium hydroxide 71, 109
potassium iodide 175
potassium nitrate 170
potassium permanganate,
        decomposition of 62
precipitate 66
precipitation 22, 66
pressure 26–9
    atmospheric 28–9
    boiling 29
    changes of state and 27–8
    on ice 27
    on other planets 28
    standard 28
Priestley, Joseph 87–8, 112
products 57, 58
propanone 37, 42
protons 52, 54
Proust, Joseph 51, 52
purity, testing for 32
PVC (polyvinyl chloride) 133
Pyrex glass 6
pyroclastic bombs 93

quartz 96, 97
quicklime 60

radiation 125, 153
radioactive materials 91, 125, 161
raindrops 22
Ramsay, William 78
raw materials 140–5
reactants 57
reactivity series 107, 110–11
recycling 164, 165
reduction 65
relative atomic mass (RAM) 168
renewable materials 163–5

research laboratory 13
residue 40
rhodium 159
robot gnat 16
rock
    igneous 95–7, 98
    metamorphic 98–9
    sedimentary 97–8, 100
    types 95–9
    weathering of 97, 99–101
rock cycle 91, 101–3
rock salt 98
rubidium 170
rust 89–90, 119,132

salt 51, 70
sandstone 97, 100
saturated solutions 36, 41
sediment 39
sedimentary rock 97–8, 100
separating funnel 46
shale 99
shield volcanoes 94
sieves 39
silicates 92
silicon 92
silicon crystals 81
silicon oxide 127
silver 56, 96, 122–3
silver bromide 174–5
silver chloride 62, 66
silver glance 122
silver nitrate 66
slag 127
slaked lime 60
slate 99
smelting 150–1
smog 156
smoke particles, physical removal of 158
smokeless fuel 158
snowflakes 22
sodium 56, 169–70
    extraction by electrolysis 116, 118
    properties 51
    reaction with oxygen 107
    reaction with water 108
sodium aluminate 131
sodium aluminium fluoride 131
sodium chloride 105, 114, 115, 116, 118, 177
sodium fluoride 174
sodium hydrogencarbonate 75
sodium hydroxide 71, 72, 108, 169
    manufacture 142
    solution 115
    uses 142
soil 34, 37
solder 126
solid/gas mixtures 34

solid/liquid mixtures 34
solid/solid mixtures 34
    separating 37–8
solids 15
    forces of attraction in 23
    pressure in 26
    properties 16
solubility 36
solubility curve 36
soluble gas/solid 36
solute 35
solute/solvent mixture
    separating solute from 41–2
    separating solvent from 43–4
solution 34, 35–7, 115
    saturated 36, 41
solvent
    liquids and gases in 36–7
    separating from solute/solvent mixture
        43–4
    water as universal 37
soot 153, 156
sphalerite 130
Spooncer, Rachel 140
Stahl, Georg 86
stainless steel 130
state symbols 179
steam 21
steel 89, 129–30, 131
stratosphere 77
strontium 56, 172
sub-atomic particles 52
sublimation 21–2, 26
sulphur 106, 136–7
sulphur dioxide 87, 136–7
    as air pollution 101, 153, 155
    chemical removal of 157–8
    production of 106, 141
sulphur pump 136–7
sulphur trioxide, production of 141
sulphur vapour 22
sulphuric acid 70, 115, 155, 176
    manufacture 67, 137, 164
    production of 101, 141
    uses 142
superphosphate 142
surface area and reaction speed 67
suspension 34
synthesis 64, 105

tare 4
tarnishing 123
teaching laboratories 12
temperature and reaction speed 67
Thales 19
thermometer 3, 4–5
tin 90
titanium 142

top loading balance 3, 4
triangle of fire 85–6
trinitrotoluene (TNT) 145
troposphere 77

ultraviolet radiation 153
universal indicator 73, 74
uranium 56, 91
uranus 28

vacuum packaging 90
vanadium oxide 141
vinegar 70
volcanoes 93–4, 103
Volta, Alessandro 112–13
voltaic pile 113

voltmeter 111
volume 15, 16
vulcanised rubber 137

warning signs 12
water 19, 20
    changing state of 22–3
    decomposition 63
    distilled 41
    in fire fighting 86
    oxygen in 37
    reactions of metals with 107–9
    super-heated 136
    testing for purity 32
    as universal solvent 37
    vapour 22, 62
water cycle 22, 23

water pollution 159–61
    fresh water 159–60
    sea water 160–1
weathering of rock 97, 99
white spirit 37
women chemical engineers 140
word equations 57, 176
wrought iron 128

xenon 78, 82

yeast 66

zinc 89, 109, 130
zinc blende 130
zinc oxides 62
zinc plating 90